**The British surrender
of Hong Kong
25th December 1941**

CAPTIVE YEARS

CAPTIVE YEARS

Japanese soldier silhouetted against Victoria Peak, Hong Kong island

CAPTIVE YEARS

The Occupation of Hong Kong · 1941–45

Alan Birch & Martin Cole

Heinemann Asia

Hong Kong • Singapore • Kuala Lumpur

HEINEMANN EDUCATIONAL BOOKS (ASIA) LTD
Yik Yin Building, 321–3 To Kwa Wan Road,
Kowloon, Hong Kong
41 Jalan Pemimpin, Singapore 2057
No. 2, Jalan 20/16A, Paramount Garden,
Petaling Jaya, Selangor, Malaysia

Heinemann Educational Books Ltd., London
Associated companies, branches &
representatives throughout the world

ISBN 962-225-082-3

Typesetting by Graphicraft Typesetters, Hong Kong
Printed in Hong Kong by
Dah Hua Printing Press Co., Ltd.
26, Lee Chung St., 9/F, Chaiwan, H.K.

Contents

Illustrations

Liberation
(pages 159 — 169)

Foreword

The series of radio programmes on which this book is based was planned as a sequel to an earlier series *Captive Christmas*, in which an attempt was made to recapture the individual experiences of the people who were caught up in the battle for Hong Kong in those fateful days of December 1941.

There was a definite end to that Christmas catastrophe which overtook the Colony with the surrender of the Governor, Sir Mark Young, as Commander-in-Chief of the Allied Forces, to General Sakai, Commander of the Imperial Japanese Armies.

But history must conform to life. First, life must go on and — more painful than any single shock — the agony of recovery must be endured. That is the overall impression of life in Hong Kong in the years of enemy occupation after Christmas 1941.

Moveover, life is different from history too: history is the recounting of experiences which have a conclusion. In the case of Hong Kong, the history of the years 1941-1945 is like a fairy story with a happy ending — the eventual defeat of Japan and the liberation of the Colony by a task force of British naval forces.

But, as we search the memories of the survivors of that era of anguish, and recreate their thoughts and feelings through the medium of interviews and reminiscences, we cannot but realize that at the time there was no outcome in sight. If many people claimed the certainty of the hope of inevitable victory, it was also true that in the dark days of 1942 and 1943 it was far from easy to look into the future and penetrate the clouds of despair and doubt.

We are deeply indebted to those brave souls who were willing to re-experience the trials and ordeals of that terrible period in Hong Kong's history. Sometimes this was not possible. The effort for some to cast their minds back to their own suffering, or more often, the suffering and death of their friends and dear ones, was too painful. We, as chroniclers of those times, could not insist upon tears and nightmares even if our purpose was to remind the people of Hong Kong today of the debt owed to all those who, willingly or unwillingly, underwent that ordeal in order that Hong Kong be the place it is today.

There was at least one occasion when, reading the diaries and letters of an inmate of Stanley, it seemed that we were probing too deeply if we revealed the pain and despair experienced by one person in his captivity.

Radio programmes cannot be produced without voices. There were, however, times for silence. This book, which attempts to retain some of the immediacy of the radio presentation in these recollections, is dedicated to all those Hong Kong belongers who experienced this traumatic period in the history of Hong Kong. If there is sometimes a case for silence, the sacrifices of these citizens should not be forgotten.

ALAN BIRCH

Note on the Radio Series

It would have been very fitting to preface these chapters with a list of characters whose observations, reminiscences and comments were used in the compilation of the thirteen broadcasts. However, one very compelling practical consideration prevented this. Many survivors of this period were interviewed and recorded for this series and they are identified either before or after each quotation in the transcripts. Use was also made of R.T.H.K. and B.B.C. archival tapes. Unfortunately, in the course of the preparation of the programmes these tapes were damaged as historical records. Consequently, whilst these impressions, given many years ago, may be sharper and possibly more accurate because they were nearer to the event, they suffer, in most cases, from being anonymous. Wherever possible, when the voice of an individual could be identified the speaker's name has been supplied.

It was the intention of the producer of this series not to limit it to readings of written accounts of the captive years, and an attempt was made to make the programmes as kaleidoscopic as possible in order to produce more of a totality of feeling. I hope, therefore, that those kind and helpful persons who co-operated in this series will not expect to see their names mentioned separately as in the programme of a stage drama. Nevertheless, I should like to acknowledge their assistance, without which the series could not have been compiled.

The radio series was first broadcast by Radio Television Hong Kong from 23 December 1979 to 16 March 1980.

1 The Surrender
25 December 1941

Thanks for the memory
Of forming up in twos
When lining up in queues,
And disappointment felt
In tasting Stanley stew,
How lovely it was . . .

— Stanley Internment Camp Song

Four members of the Hong Kong Volunteers remember 25 December 1941.

Colonel Bothelo:

❛I knew that Hong Kong had surrendered when a despatch rider by
the name of Billy Poi came to my headquarters to say they had been
driving through Wanchai and had seen troops discarding and
breaking their rifles. My immediate feeling was one of grave
disappointment because I had believed and had been told to teach
my troops that we would fight to the last man, to the last bullet. So
to be told to capitulate was a serious blow to me.❜

Bombardier Weller:

❛We were then recalled to a line on O'Brien Road and we were told
that this was a holding action on our part, as the last line of defence
was being dug at the junction of Arsenal Street and Queen's Road
East. While we were there we could see in the distance the Japanese
coming around Canal Road, peeping around the corners, running
behind pillars and generally advancing up. At that stage, an officer
came along with a very large table-cloth or bedsheet tied to a
bamboo pole, and said, "That's all chaps, the war's ended."❜

Private Gomez:

> ‘ We were in the pill boxes around the Mount Davis area. Our job was to guard the Kennedy cross-roads and when the order came through for the surrender we laid down our arms and marched to St John's Place where we congregated. As far as I can recollect we were all served with what rations were available. We heard that our colours were being buried somewhere around the area. ’

Private Remedios:

> ‘ I was perhaps very naive at the time. I thought that Hong Kong would be fought for until the last soldier died. We would be a sort of Tobruk in the Far East. ’

The battle for Hong Kong, that brief eighteen-day affray in December 1941, had never been the defence of an impregnable fortress. The defence lines had been quickly pierced by the unorthodox thrusts of the Japanese invaders, and in effect the aftermath was no more than a series of bloody skirmishes of mopping up between the Japanese and isolated pockets of resistance. For General Maltby, Commander of this ever dwindling garrison, the pressure of the military position could only dictate one reasonable line of action. But, for the Governor, Sir Mark Young, escape from the dilemma between honour and surrender was not so easy. Only in these last dying throes of the battle could he bring an end to these futile sacrifices. As he wrote in retrospect:

> ‘ There was now no room for postponement of the decision which I was called upon to take without involving the General's head-quarters in hand to hand fighting. There was now no other possible course open to me but to exercise the discretion which a recent telegram of yours has authorized me to use when further resistance ceased to be possible. ’

The General and the Governor crossed the harbour in a Japanese launch bound for the Peninsula Hotel, the Japanese army headquarters.

‘I told General Sakai that we had crossed the lines only in consequence of the threat that an attack would be launched if we did not do so. We were asked whether this cessation of resistance was unconditional and I replied that I had made no conditions.’

Phyllis Harrop, who was with the police and still in touch with Government House, anxiously noted in her diary for that unforgettable Christmas Day:

‘Everybody is very depressed and we are all wondering what is going to happen next. Our fears are of the worst. The Governor has not returned from Kowloon and has declared himself a prisoner.’

Gwen Priestwood, who was also close to things, was told about the scene at the Peninsula:

‘One officer, who had witnessed the surrender, said that Sir Mark himself had been almost physically sick.’

Government broadcaster, John Stericker, describes the anxiety of those tense hours:

‘Somebody told me they'd just come down from Government House and they were disconsolately sitting around the Government House drawing-room. Captain Battye-Smith, who was the Governor's ADC, was going around asking people not to drop cigarette ash on the Governor's carpet.’

In the Peninsula Hotel, on the other side of the Harbour, the Governor was now an unwilling guest obeying a different set of house rules.

‘I was kept in solitary confinement in a suite of rooms at the Peninsula Hotel for a period of seven weeks. I had an interview with General Sakai on the morning of December 26 and was informed by him that I should be allowed to live in a house in Hong Kong until orders concerning me came from Tokyo. But in fact, after that day, I was given no opportunity of leaving the room in which I was confined and my repeated complaints and requests for information were completely ignored until the middle of January. I was then interviewed by another Japanese General who informed me that my request for information about our casualties could not be granted; that I could not be allowed to see any other prisoners; that I should be provided with such articles of clothing etc. as were necessary; and finally that I must realize that the English were a defeated nation and that I must be obedient. On February 19 I was removed by air to Shanghai. **9**

General Maltby was apparently taken back to Flagstaff House where, that evening, stealing into the garden under cover of darkness, he and a Lieutenant McGregor, his ADC, buried the colours of the two regiments — the First Middlesex and 2/14 Punjabis — to prevent them from falling into the hands of the victorious Japanese. Sad to relate, these regimental trophies have completely disappeared and every attempt to find the buried treasure in Flagstaff House garden has failed. Some rescue operations carried out that day of surrender, however, turned out more successfully. In the afternoon, Admiral Chan Chak and a party of other officers, who would have been summarily executed by the Japanese, escaped from Aberdeen.

Captain Freddie Guest, the liaison officer on the Admiral's staff, recalls:

6 We reached the fourth floor and MacMillan, who had been here once before, quickly recognized the door and gave it a rather soft tap. It had to be soft because we didn't want them to think it was the Japs already. The door was gently opened by a Chinaman who was none other than Henry Hsu, the Admiral's right-hand man, whom we had both met on several occasions. He looked relieved and quickly let us in. Then he took us into a room where Admiral Chan Chak was sitting at the desk. There was another Chinese with him, Colonel Yee. We greeted the Admiral and he motioned each of us to a chair. Peter MacMillan opened the conversation.

"Well, Admiral," he began, "I suppose you've heard the news?"

He nodded. "Why are you here?" he asked. "I did not expect to see you so soon."

MacMillan grinned and went on. "The Japs are moving into the town faster than we thought," he said, "and unless we get out of here right away, it may be too difficult later. The patrols are stopping everybody. We thought of trying to get through to Aberdeen and hide up somewhere and see if we can contact the Motor Torpedo Boats tonight. Our plans are rather sketchy but there it is. Do you feel it's worth taking a chance with us?"

The Admiral was in ordinary Chinese clothes and carried a very small hold-all with him. Henry Hsu his right-hand man, a most likable fellow, was also in Chinese clothes and also carried a small hold-all. Colonel Yee was in Chinese clothes and carried a bag. MacMillan and myself both still wore British uniform and carried just a few things we had been able to lay our hands on in our pockets. On the face of it, it didn't look promising. But I had already convinced myself that the possible results justified the risks. We got downstairs and took a look out. All there was to see was more and more bewildered crowds of Chinese moving to and fro like lost sheep and Japanese soldiers everywhere pushing their way through in the most arrogant and cocky manner. It looked hopeless and I turned to the others to see if I could guess what they were thinking. Henry Hsu just leaned towards us and said, "Wait, I go and look." He'd been gone only a few minutes when he suddenly appeared at the entrance with an old motor car, a four-seater Austin with a canvas top. It was like a conjuring trick and I felt like applauding as I would have applauded Houdini. The "magician" got out and ran to where we were standing and told us briefly that he had found the car just around one of the side streets. We asked him about petrol and he said he didn't know how much was in it but it had started and that was good enough for him. Then he beckoned us to the car and he and the Admiral climbed into the front seats. Colonel Yee, MacMillan and myself got into the back and quickly got down out of sight. Then the car started and with a loud blast of the horn we were away. Once or twice our hearts beat faster as Jap patrols were at the point of stopping us but Henry just shouted something at them and they got out of the way. When I asked him later what he'd said to them, he told me that he had just shouted "Banzai" and "Long live the Emperor" in Japanese and this apparently did the trick. Once we had got away from the waterfront, things appeared to get much easier except that the Jap patrols looked more dangerous. We reached a bend in the road and a Japanese NCO stepped into the road to stop us. Henry just slowed down and, as the man stepped aside, he put his foot down on the accelerator and shot past him. As the car careered round the bend we heard his shots. I can't say I felt too happy about it as we were in the back and likely to be the first casualties. However, we had no further incidents and finally reached the harbour at Aberdeen. **9**

The plan was for a small fleet of motor torpedo boats to sneak out of the harbour there and to make for free China via Mirs Bay. But only a 25-foot motor launch could be found at the rendezvous. Guest continues:

6 At last we cleared the harbour mouth and headed due south into the channel running between the peninsula of Stanley, away to the east, and Brickhill Point on the west. The channel widened rapidly the further we cruised and we were soon leaving Brickhill point behind us. I looked round into the cabin of our boat and noticed that everyone appeared to be settling down to snooze as the little engine throbbed out its monotonous and dreary note. At the time I was sitting at the feet of the helmsman and advising him to steer closer to the west side of the channel. I was still uncertain as to whether the Japs had, by that time, completely occupied the Stanley peninsula or not, and thought it safer to run closer to the island of Lok Ma Chau, which was now away to the west. We had now left the harbour well behind us and the channel had widened still more. It was all very quiet except for the throb of the engine and I was beginning to think we were safe — at least from the land — when suddenly through the stillness of that lovely evening there came a crack of a single shot quickly followed by another and in the next second came the frightening rattle of a machine gun. Everybody looked dazed and then I decided that the game was up and that our only chance was to swim for it.

I was very very thankful when at last we reached the island and

I was able to pull myself up onto the rocks. There was no beach at this spot and it was indeed an effort to climb out of the water. Fortunately I was able to help out the others, including the Admiral, who had made the swim completely unaided. He'd managed it with only one leg and a bullet wound in the arm. He was minus his left leg and wounded in his left arm so was completely unbalanced and quite incapable of moving around without help. Altogether five of us had landed at this particular spot — the Admiral, Henry Hsu, Bill Robinson, MacMillan and myself. Goring, Macdougall and Oxford had landed a little distance away to our left. Thus, there were now only six British and two Chinese. We never saw the others again. **'**

The survivors fell into an exhausted sleep on this little island and then the MTBs, arriving late, appeared on the scene. The survivors, being taken for Japanese, were fired upon by these navy vessels, and Captain Guest had to take another swim.

' As I swam, my thoughts turned somehow to England and to my family and I remember thinking what a hell of a long way it was and if I'd ever see it or them again. This thought, trite though it may have been, spurred me on. I was now getting somewhere near that confounded MTB and, as my eyes had got thoroughly used to the darkness, could see a naval rating on guard, pacing slowly up and down the small deck. Under his arm he was carrying a tommy gun at the ready and his finger was suspiciously near the trigger. Suddenly I had a horrible feeling that if I shouted out he would probably let fly with his gun first and ask questions after. So I made up my mind to be damned careful and swam very quietly right close to the boat. I then let out some good plain English cuss words which only an Englishman could say, and only a British sailor would understand. It certainly had the desired effect. He gave a quick start, leaned over the side and said, "Who the bloody hell are you?" I just answered, "For Christ's sake, pick me up," and with that he bent over and heaved me on board. **'**

The MTBs returned cautiously to the island. There they found the Admiral and his party. Later, on board one of the MTBs, it was decided to make a dash for Mirs Bay. This mainly naval party was successful and these escapees quickly found their way to Waichow, a pocket of resistance against the occupying forces in Southern Kwangtung, a few days later. But at Stanley, even after the ceasefire order, the battle continued and some were not so lucky.

Among these last defenders of Hong Kong was Bombardier Weller.

> ‹ I was a gunner in first battery of the Hong Kong Volunteers. We had previously been situated at Cape D'Aguilar and when the Japanese landed we had to blow up our guns and retreat to Stanley. We were there from December 19th until Christmas Eve when we were told to stand by and had to move down into Stanley, not in the village itself actually but in a line behind St Stephen's College. This was about eight o'clock at night and we were told we were the second line of defence and that we didn't have too much to worry about. Well anyway, round about ten, we were in a line behind St Stephen's College, overlooking a football field with two friends. About midnight a terrific racket started in the village and tracers were flashing through the treetops. There was a lot of activity and this went on all through the night. Of course what we didn't realize was that our platoon in the centre and on the right had fallen back, so in the morning, first.light — this was Christmas morning — we suddenly realized that we were completely surrounded. ›

News of the cease-fire, official or unofficial, did not reach Brigadier Wallis's beleaguered troops on the Stanley peninsula for some twenty-four hours and, as a most awful epilogue to the drama which was now supposed to have come to an end, a bloody and ferocious battle was still being fought, bringing atrocity and agony to the last defenders of Hong Kong. Bombardier Weller continues:

> ‹ So there was only one thing to do and that was to pull back to Barton's bungalow which was on the corner overlooking the football field. We made a break for it, reached the bungalow, and we were on the lawn outside. We eventually had to retreat inside when it got

too hot for us there and there wasn't any way we could get out. We knew we were cut off completely, and eventually the Japanese rushed the bungalow and then of course they brought up a flame-thrower and there wasn't much you could do about that. They flushed everybody out. I, fortunately, managed to get the door shut and in the flames and smoke I managed to get my gas mask on and that, I think, saved me. I managed to stay where I was, but the rest in the bungalow were all bayoneted as they came out in flames. **'**

The Japanese stormed St Stephen's College, now being used as a field hospital and, inflamed to blood lust because they had been fired on by troops sheltering in the grounds, bayoneted the helpless patients in their beds, shot and bayoneted the doctors and raped the nurses. As Bombardier Weller knew, those fighting on could expect no mercy. It must have been painful for Weller to recall the anxious hours of that night.

' As the day wore on I began to think that maybe I had a chance. Anyway in the afternoon, at about two o'clock or three I think it was, the Canadians counter-attacked from Stanley Fort. I heard them coming. I was a bit worried because, you know, if I dashed out they might mistake me for a Jap. So I called out that I was a volunteer and a voice from somewhere shouted out, you know, Middlesex. I then discovered that there were two chaps in the next room who had also survived, though they were badly burnt. They quickly joined me, and then of course the Japanese counter-attacked and before we could join up with the Canadians, they were driven back with heavy casualties. So I had these two chaps with me, a Corporal and a Private from the Middlesex. We were all in one room now and we stayed through the day and through the night and the chap who was very badly burnt — his face was just one big blister — kept going to sleep, snoring. I had to stop him from doing that, and in the end he got pretty fed up with this and said, "Well, I'm going," and so we decided that if he was going, we'd better all go. So off we went. We took our boots off and crawled across the lawn and down the bank. Unfortunately we ran into a Japanese patrol. We managed to give them the slip in the darkness and decided the only thing we could do was to go back to the bungalow, which we did. There we spent a very uncomfortable night, because it was a very small room, just a sort of washroom, until the following morning.'

There was a small irony here, because the turmoil of those last confused hours of battle brought liberty to a small group of Japanese civilians who had been rounded up when war broke out on 8 December and put in Stanley gaol for their protection. Nambu San of the Japanese Mitsui Company recalls their fear and excitement on that Christmas night:

'At early morning on the 25th, a hand-to-hand battle began near the prison. The lawn in the garden of the house, which was located north-west of the prison, caught fire from a grenade. On the hill just in front of the prison gate there were two houses held by British troops. Grenades were repeatedly thrown into the houses by the Japanese soldiers and they exploded with a roar. They finally occupied the houses, all of us watching these brave actions of the Japanese soldiers through the prison windows. We were very much excited as well as grateful to the soldiers. We were sure that the occupation of Hong Kong would be near at hand. We were liberated on the night of the 25th. At about two o'clock in the afternoon that day, the prison buildings were hit by a number of bullets. The missionaries were so scared that they said to us, "Tell the Japanese forces not to shoot here, since there are Japanese in this prison compound. They may not be aware that you are here." We replied to them: "We can't say such nonsense. If they have to attack here in order to occupy the Stanley Gun Fort, we are willing to be sacrificed. How can we Japanese say such a ridiculous thing?"'

Their spell of imprisonment was brief and now they were liberated. Nambu continues his account:

'An army major said, "Hello, Nambu," stretching out his hand. I found he was Ota, who was in Hong Kong until September. We took each other's hands and shared this joy of unexpected reunion. I was told the British forces at this headquarters had surrendered and a staff officer, Hosukowa, was there with the British Colonel, to persuade the commander at the Stanley Fort also to surrender. The staff officer, Hosukowa, introduced me to the Commander, Major Hirashira, who served us some canned pineapples and whisky. We overheard soldiers reporting to the Commander that there was heavy fighting in the area. After experiencing various other memorable incidents, we went back to the prison around 2300 hrs., being accompanied by Lieutenant Shimizu of the Military Police. There was no moon that night but stars were all over the sky, twinkling. It was dead quiet and I thought I heard some insects singing. **'**

When great calamities bring the routine of ordinary life to a standstill, it is the minor experiences, and sometimes the incongruities between the tragic and even humorous circumstances of the moment which live on in the mind. John Stericker, the broadcaster, remembers how his civilian boss reacted to the news of the surrender down in Central:

> **'** I looked out of the ante-room window of the studio and saw the police loading their rifles onto trucks. So I went up to Mr Wynn-Jones, the Postmaster General, who was asleep in a chair — we were all without sleep, of course with this constant bombing and shelling. I woke him up and I said, "Sir, we've surrendered," and he leapt up. He was a very bad-tempered chap and he said, "John, you're under arrest." People around him were sure that, as we were all likely to be under arrest at any minute, one more wouldn't make much difference. **'**

Soon it would be impossible to make that kind of joke. The silence of the city came not only from the now cold guns and the dead. There was an unnatural stillness and foreboding, shared by everyone, over what the immediate future would bring. The defeated had come face to face with the conqueror.

2 The Aftermath

For centuries the victors of war, in the aftermath of battle, have imposed their wanton will upon the unfortunate inhabitants of captured cities, rich in wealth, wine and women. Now it was the turn of Hong Kong to experience that ordeal. Moreover, giving vent to a long restrained envy of the luxurious life of the Taipans, the Chinese also tried to take their toll of the loot which was there for the picking.

Paul Tsui, then a student at the university, remembers:

> ‘I was actually lodging in my sister's place at Mosque Street, near Robinson Road. We could see looters carrying all sorts of items continuously, like ants, coming down the Peak. The looting started at that time when all the mansions up at the Peak were evacuated because the houses were not occupied: everybody just helped themselves.’

Already the dead lying in the streets would receive no respect. A corpse was a corpse and his clothes could be put to use to keep the cold and hungry warm. An unnamed Chinese spectator recalls:

> ‘I looked out of my verandah this morning and I saw the body of a man slumped in a heap in the middle of the road, right in front of our house. The street was full of pedestrians, many of whom would come cover and take a look at the body, to see if it was anyone they knew. One man walked off with the dead man's woollen hat. Another absconded with his shoes and yet another stripped the body of its overcoat. Suddenly a man stepped forward from the crowd. He must have recognized the dead man because he carried the body to the side of the road. Then he hurriedly scribbled characters on a slip of paper which he placed on the body and then weighed it down with two stones. The paper read: "The body will be privately collected." This was done because the man realized the Japanese collection van might come and remove it.’

16

There was swift and grim retribution when the Japanese caught these people helping themselves. John Stericker was shocked at the brutal treatment meted out to the local population.

> It was really rather awful, because when we went past the lower Peak Tram station — there were some trees there then — tied to each tree were three strings, like beads, of Chinese. I suppose they had been caught looting. The rope was tied to the tree at one end, then it was looped around the neck of a Chinese, then with another three feet looped around the neck of the next one, right down the line. I'm afraid we had to go past them again later and of course as one dropped from exhaustion he pulled another down and there they were left to die. I know a friend of mine saw an old Chinese woman and a girl scraping up rice that had fallen off a truck and the Japanese immediately shot them and pushed them into the water.

The Japanese of course took what they wanted — the right of the conqueror. Dr Li Shu-fan describes the pillaging of Hong Kong:

> Throughout the three-day celebration, Japanese soldiers strolled up and down the streets of the city, stopping cars and commanding the drivers to take them for joy rides. They seized whatever they wanted from stores, especially from the wine and clothing shops, sometimes tossing a few military notes on the counter in any quantity they liked. If a store was locked they broke in and helped themselves freely. On the night after Christmas I looked into the Shan Kwang hotel windows across the road from the hospital and saw Japanese soldiers dining, singing, drinking and dancing with one another. Parties like this swelled to orgies throughout Hong Kong. It seemed as though the soldiers had been specifically given licence to commit any act they wished. Their first thought was to put wine in their bellies, then they set out for excitement and mischief under the pretext of searching for arms or suspects. They broke into house after house at the point of a gun. Once in, they slapped, kicked, murdered, stole and raped. Throughout the night we heard people

wailing and crying in the distance, "Save life, save life," and the desperate beating of hundreds of gongs, tins and cans. The whole of Happy Valley rang from end to end with these pleas for help. **'**

Dr Li Shu-fan was able, with the help of the Indian watchman at the hospital, to divert the sex-hungry marauders away from his nursing staff. But in the street any woman was potential prey. Local inhabitant Mrs Lee remembers to this day:

> **'** One soldier hauled and pushed a woman up the stairs to the bedroom. Half way up the stairs this woman knelt down and pleaded with the soldier, patting her big pregnant stomach and saying to him, "Baby, baby." **'**

Miss Hui, a young student at that time, recalls:

> **'** When they entered people's homes they would take whatever they fancied. They often asked for watches or clocks or even young girls, who were usually not available, as people were well aware of this and had already found safe hiding places for their daughters. **'**

The wife of a Chinese doctor also tells of a desperate stratagem adopted by a girl to put off attempts at rape.

> **'** One of the soldiers picked on an amah, who was in her middle thirties, but little did he know how well she had planned to save herself in such a predicament. She was wearing a sanitary pad stained with mercurochrome, knowing that Japanese, like all eastern men, regard a menstruating woman as unclean and therefore will not touch her. She was so right, she got away with it. **'**

The threat of rape was a constant worry for women of whatever race, although Emily Hahn said she put on a brave face.

> **'** "What happened?" Suzie stared at me and said, "Rape!" I said to myself, nonsense, it doesn't really happen. I also said rape is

impossible unless of course you are using a sandbag or a bayonet. I said to myself, I won't be taken in by those horror stories. No! No! No! I'll hold on to myself, I said. If I'm raped I won't care. It won't be my fault and will mean nothing. It's like being wounded. **>**

And a certain Mrs Angus, a friend of Emily's, even managed to make a joke of it.

< Mrs Angus, a venerable lady of sixty-five, sent us into hysterical giggles by reporting that one of the soldiers had made advances to her. It was the truth. He had pointed to a couch and then made an unmistakable gesture. Mrs Angus was the only female in all our crowd who had been approached disrespectfully. "It's my figure that gets 'em," she said. **>**

Less dangerous was the childlike desire of the Japanese private to possess himself of as many wristwatches as possible. It was extremely unwise to answer the artless question, 'What time is it?.' Emily Hahn, who well knew the Japanese ways, tells of one encounter of this kind.

< Just as we left the hospital grounds, a few yards from the gate, two Japanese came along. One was a private and the other, since he was carrying a sword, must have been an officer. The private hailed us: "Oi!" We pretended not to hear. He yelled louder, angrily. We stopped. My eyes met Suzie's. She sat down suddenly on a rock. The officer grinned and walked off so he couldn't see us. The private approached us at a run and motioned that he wanted to look at our arms. It was our wristwatches he wanted, not our virtue. The relief of it made me shaky in the knees. What's more, he missed my watch — I wear it on the right wrist and he didn't look for it there under my leather jacket. As he took the watches from the others, Suzie found the nerve to say, "You have one already." She touched it lightly. "Shame," said Suzie banteringly. The private grinned awkwardly. He hung his head and grinned like a naughty schoolboy showing his great teeth like battered tombstones — but he took the watches. **>**

This scene was repeated a countless number of times in Hong Kong, and those who had a home left intact were wise to stay out of sight. Dr Lee, a private practitioner, was at Queen Mary Hospital, which had been swamped with people seeking treatment for their injuries incurred during the shelling and the air-raids. Now the stream of wounded had completely dried up.

> ‘I was working in the Casualty Department and after the surrender of Hong Kong, there was practically no work for me to do because nobody in Hong Kong would ever dare to go out.’

Of course some had to, to seek refuge with friends or to try to look after their own property which, if left unwatched, would have been stripped bare by the soldier and civilian ants.

Mr Chan Siu Jin, now a senior Hong Kong Government civil servant, then a boy, remembers:

> ‘All nine of us, including my parents, were taking refuge in a friend's house in Village Road, Happy Valley. Of course, certain parts of Happy Valley were heavily bombarded by the Japanese. One thing that left a very deep impression on me was that a lot of Canadians, Indians and Hong Kong Chinese soldiers were retreating from across the area around Blue Pool Road towards the waterfront. They kept on shouting slogans and what not when they passed through our house in Village Road. My father, a civil servant then, and also a member of the Special Constabulary Police, was with us. He was armed with one pistol and went out and rounded up five or six rickshaws. It was a very surprising thing then because Hong Kong was already at war yet rickshaws were still running. Probably that was the only means of public transport available. We loaded as much clothing and personal effects as possible into these rickshaws and then members of the family took the rickshaws back to our old house in Lockhart Road. I can still remember the number of our place — it was 446 Lockhart Road. All our chattels and personal effects were left in that house in Lockhart Road. Of course they were all stolen. Those robbers and burglars really did a very thorough job and took virtually everything, lock, stock and barrel.’

Life was now reduced to providing the basic necessities and, as S.J. Chan explains, this involved further sacrifices for his father, an educated man and a lover of books.

> ‘ Well, the first thing that we had to do, I remember, was to stay indoors. We had to start a fire to cook a meal and the only fuel available was the books that we had. Because my father was somewhat of a scholar he had lots and lots of books. Funnily enough we started with tearing off pages from the *Encyclopedia Britannica*. It took us quite a few pages before we could start the kettle boiling and finally make a pot of tea. ’

Of course, there were some signs of the daily routine of peace-time, which had been so violently disrupted only a short time previously, reasserting themselves. The leading Chinese newspaper, the *Wah Kiu Yat Po*, appeared on Boxing Day with the bland announcement that 'The Japanese army occupied the whole of Hong Kong at 6 p.m. yesterday'. This angered one Chinese who had recently arrived in Hong Kong.

> ‘ Their tone was so dispassionate that readers must suspect the publishers of being cold-blooded. The *Wah Kiu Yat Po* may see itself as reporting objectively, but Japan is not just England's enemy but also China's enemy. These fascist assaults have made them the enemy of mankind and justice. How can they be so oblivious to the cruelty meted out around them unless it is to protect their self-interests? ’

It was the ever-present anxieties of encountering the Japanese and the immediate pressing daily necessities of life which preoccupied people, who had become refugees almost in their own homes. Marion Dudley had found shelter upon the Peak in a group of about thirty people camping out in a civil servant's home.

> ‘ Our men kept guard all night but no one came but the dog from the K.S.s' home. The men went on a reconnoitering tour and came back to say all was quiet on the Peak. We decided to try for home. That

was a queer cavalcade — the two cars making a sandwich with the thirty people, so that they would not be so easily confiscated. The children were played up prominently as they are always well treated by the soldiers. Our main thought was, what will happen when we meet the first Japanese? Such a silent smoking city we looked down into as we slowly circled around down the road — empty harbour, empty streets. A car went by full of Japanese officers who stared through us as if we were ghosts. **'**

In fact the Japanese often surprised their captives by friendly gestures, especially towards children.

There was clearing up to be done everywhere. Some of the damage and litter would still be there at the end of the war, awaiting the British on their return in 1945. To prevent epidemics from the polluted water supplies and to safeguard the health of their own troops, it was necessary for the Japanese to collect the dead and the dying from the city streets and the more distant hillsides. Bombardier Weller was at Stanley:

> **'** We had a look out and saw Japanese with our people picking up dead bodies. Then, suddenly, one of the Japanese tried the door, came in and saw us. He was a bit annoyed that they had overlooked us, but still, we realized then that the surrender had taken place and it was all over. They had us picking up our own dead. My two friends were both killed. **'**

The clearing up of the battle fields went on for days. Phyllis Harrop recorded the post-battle accounting in these words:

> **'** Lists of casualties are gradually coming in but so far no news of those who were trapped at Repulse Bay, Stanley and North Point areas and who disappeared before the surrender. There are hundreds of names missing and without help from the Japs we cannot compile correct lists. **'**

In this strange interval of confusion, the vacuum created by the absence of the police made it necessary for the Japanese authorities to rely upon the Hong

Kong civil servants as well. Phyllis Harrop describes how, on 29 December, she went to see Mr Gimson, the Colonial Secretary, now in charge of the war-wrecked administration. The Governor of course was a prisoner and held incommunicado in Kowloon.

> ‘ This morning I went over to Prince's Building to make contact with the new Colonial Secretary, Mr Gimson. I had already met him once but only for a short moment when he visited us at Police Head-quarters. Poor man — he arrived on the afternoon of December 7th. What a dismal mess he stepped into! All staff from Government House have been moved down to Prince's Building under orders from the Japanese. They need help and so I have stayed and worked with them. They're compiling lists for the Japanese of Kowloon residents who wish to return — not English people however. Everything is at a standstill. ’

Government House was now occupied by Japanese officers. Sub-Lieutenant Bush, who only a year earlier had been teaching at a Japanese University and who had brought a Japanese wife back with him to Hong Kong, was pressed into service as an interpreter during an interrogation of General Maltby by a Japanese Colonel. He describes this occasion when the General was making his last effort to save the British and Canadian soldiers and nurses from the wrath of the enemy:

> ‘ Government House, situated a short way up the Peak from the city, was surrounded with Japanese sentries. It was in semi-darkness. There was no electricity and our General, with twenty or so other senior army and naval officers, were together in a lounge which was bathed in the soft light of candles. It was a heart-rending meeting. For me, one of the most tragic and impressive moments of my life because of the nobility and dignity of those senior officers. We were joined by a Japanese Colonel. The General asked if it was the practice of the Imperial army to rape hospital nurses and shoot and bayonet the wounded in their beds. This had actually happened at North Point and at Stanley. The Japanese Colonel replied that if this were true, the culprits would be found and shot, in accordance

with military law. Some such sentence was actually carried out a few days later. **'**

Kane, Bush's wife, was later given the task of trying to trace the Scottish terrier belonging to the General's aide-de-camp, which had disappeared in the last hours of the battle. Not all was lost. Indeed there were some hopeful signs of order emerging out of the chaos. Food supplies were being organized, the city's water supply restored and emergency supplies were brought to the hospitals. Dr Selwyn-Clarke, a man of fearsome and sometimes misguided dedication to healing the sick, was largely responsible for this relief. He fortunately had some professional connection with a Japanese professor of medicine and was already exerting his influence. Charles Schafer, an American working with an airline in Hong Kong before the war, was also roped in.

> **'** Fortunately, Dr Selwyn-Clarke, a man of great vision, a great compassionate doctor with a great bedside manner had the foresight to see the need to keep the medical services going to prevent epidemics. He immediately contacted the head of the Japanese medical service and offered the full support of his staff. He asked for passes for the doctors and for the truck drivers who would supply food and fuel for the hospitals and these were granted. **'**

Dr Selwyn-Clarke was later to suffer torture and imprisonment at the hands of the Japanese, through his implication in networks of agents busy smuggling food, drugs and money into the internment camps. After the war, he was the only member of the Colonial Medical Service to become a Governor of a British Colony. He was then to write about his experiences in occupied Hong Kong.

> **'** The unburied dead lay in the streets and for months afterwards were still being found in the hills. In approximate figures, 4,000 civilians had been killed and 3,000 severely wounded. It is a picture of the ruthlessness of war and the arrogance of conquest and it was further darkened by individual brutalities. To Colonel Nagakowa and Colonel Iguchi I shall always be grateful for the chance that fell to me during the first fifteen months of the occupation to continue my duties as best I could. It was Colonel Iguchi who secured agreement from Sir Mark Young in his detention. **'**

Now that Hong Kong was occupied, a difficult dilemma confronted many conscientious officers, as Selwyn-Clarke explains:

> ‘ The fact was that no policy to meet the circumstances of an unconditional surrender had been prepared in advance by the Hong Kong government. Left without guidance, the heads of essential services, insofar as the Japanese command might leave them any choice, would risk the charge of collaboration with the enemy if they agreed to continue any of their functions for the benefit of the community. For myself, as head of the Colony's medical department, the nature of my duties made the choice as straightforward and as binding as the Hippocratic oath. ’

Not everyone was as courageous as this man. The strains and stresses of Hong Kong's position as an occupied territory had already provoked more feelings of pessimism and naked self-interest than the nobler sentiments of sacrifice and endurance. We can only respect the fortitude of a volunteer soldier expressing, at the moment of imprisonment, the feelings of others who were less articulate:

> ‘ We had no particular feelings. There was a sense of relief that the imminent stress of war was over where we were concerned. There was a sense of frustration because we did not know what was going to happen next — a sense that we had lost our freedom and we were now just automatons to be directed to move backwards and forwards, here and there, and in a sense we were more or less slaves of the enemy. But morale was good — we did not dwell on the morbid aspects of life under these conditions. We always looked for the sunny side or we looked for the silver lining. ’

The Aftermath of the Battle

(I – VI)

I. The British surrender. A Japanese photograph of the Governor, Sir Mark Young and the G.O.C. General C.M. Maltby taken at the Peninsula Hotel. where the British surrender was signed on 25 December 1941.

This blurred photograph taken in candlelight is the only surviving record of this most historic event in the history of Hong Kong. Lieutenant General Takashi Sakai (centre) is obscured by glare from the candles.

(Winston G. Ramsey)

Saint Stephen's College
(Advance Hospital.)
4am. 25th Dec. 1941.

II. After the official surrender on Christmas Day 1941 the battle raged on at Stanley. the last defence position held by the British Forces on Hong Kong Island.
Early that morning Japanese troops stormed into St Stephen's College, being used as a forward medical station, where troops were hiding, shot one of the doctors, raped several nurses and bayonetted patients. This sketch, drawn by a doctor, Dr P.J. Barnes, is a poignant record of those atrocities committed in the last desperate hours of Hong Kong's resistance.

(A. Birch)

III. The group of fifty British and Chinese officers and men, under the command of Admiral Chan Chak, who escaped from Aberdeen on December 25th by motor torpedo boats via Mirs Bay and into Free China. They arrived at their destination, Waichow, in Kwangtung, on December 29th. This was one of the most remarkable mass escapes made from the Captured Territory throughout the three years and eight months of captivity. (*Henry H. Hsu, O.B.E.*)

IV. A group of victorious Japanese troops astride a British gun emplacement evidently shouting the cry of triumph, 'Banzai'. This was probably one of the big guns situated on the artillery fort on the summit of Mount Davis, overlooking the entrance to Victoria Harbour. (*Winston G. Ramsey*)

V. British naval personnel, with their belongings, marching down Garden Road, Central Hong Kong, under the watchful gaze of their captors.
(*Winston G. Ramsey*)

VI. All the Colony's motor vehicles which had survived the battle were collected at the site of the former Hong Kong Cricket Ground in January 1942, to be allocated for use by the occupying forces. (*Winston G. Ramsey*)

3 Civil Internment

Thanks for the memory
Of forming up in twos
When lining up in queues,
And disappointment felt
In tasting Stanley stew
How lovely it was . . .

These new words to the song, *Thanks for the Memory*, were composed in Stanley Internment Camp sometime between the years 1941 and 1945. No one would think in all seriousness of thanking the Japanese for that experience.

Dorothy Jenner who, under the pseudonymn 'Andrea', wrote the only funny book about internment, summed up the physical toll of imprisonment:

When I went into Stanley Camp in January 1942, I had black hair, I weighed about ten and a half stone. When I came out almost four years later my hair was dead white and I weighed less than six stone. I was weak and disorientated and once in town I hadn't a clue where to go or what to do.

Most of the 2,500 interned civilians — British, American, White Russians, Norwegians and others of allied nationality — suffered this physical and mental deterioration from captivity. It was a slow wearing down of nerves and bodies. The strains brought out the best and the worst — generosity and greed in this artificial wartime society.

Jean Gittins, daughter of Sir Robert Hotung, was philosophical later on about human nature in Stanley:

There's a friendly, comradely spirit that still exists which could not possibly have been generated in other ways — certainly not during normal life in Hong Kong — although it might happen amongst people who were fighting together. Another thing I think would be a tolerance, a greater tolerance towards people in general, a greater

32

breadth of mind in looking at people of all kinds, all kinds of failings, and all races.

There was a certain amount of friction, of meanness, of thieving, but there was also a great deal of generosity. It was the generosity and the basic goodness of people that impressed me most.

People who didn't do that tended to go to pieces, and generally speaking, allowing for health, I think the older people, with more mental background, managed to stand up to it better than the younger ones who were more immature.

On the whole, of course, the people who were used to a simple life stood up better. It's the people who led nice, sheltered, secure lives that suddenly just collapsed, didn't look after themselves, became dirty and neglected, and died . . . some of them.**'**

In the struggle for survival, different people reacted in different ways. Some were weak, some were strong. In this artificial culture-bed of human behaviour, traits of personality were forced into dominant strains of character. There was too much time and too little to do in this laboratory. At first, however, there was a great deal to do to make the prison and college buildings habitable. The blood stains and stench of the recent atrocities at Stanley had to be scrubbed away. Jean Gittins describes the situation:

' I found that the stories we heard of conditions in Stanley Camp were by no means exaggerated. If anything, they were a good deal worse. The accommodation was hopelessly inadequate. Thirty-five people packed into a standard-sized flat and over fifty in a small family bungalow. The flats in the Indian warders' quarters were much smaller and housed an average of seven people. The internees looked starved, despairing and utterly forlorn, although there were some who kept their spirit.**'**

'Andrea' recounts her experience at that time:

' I also found a book during those early days. I was off scouting around on my own and I came across an area where there had obviously been a lot of fighting. The place reeked of death. If you ever smell dead, rotting flesh, you never forget the smell. It's so sickly sweet it makes you gag. I could smell it for days afterwards: it was in my clothes, my hair, it even seemed to have permeated my skin. Horrible! I saw this book in the distance and I went forward to pick it up. The ground was sticky and moist and before I knew it, blood was oozing over my feet. I can't tell you what a shock that was. Not a hysterical shock, more a shatter. I picked the book up and saw that it was *Play Parade* by Noel Coward. Some of the pages were stuck together with blood, but I kept it just the same. I still have it. I had no idea at that stage of ever producing a play. It wasn't until a couple of years later when the suggestion first came up that this book was put to good use. **'**

Experience of a great calamity produces a strange paradox: it imposes an ordeal shared in common but it also heightens the individual response. This was John Stericker's reaction to the shock of internment:

' Well, I can remember what happened to me, because I had one or two friends with me. We had all come from the same hotel. We all made for St Stephen's College. I don't know why we did. Others branched off, especially the married people, to the warders' quarters because there they had beautiful houses and flats. Of course a family would settle down in one flat and say, "This is mine", and keep other people out.

Then the Japanese took a turn, especially when they rounded up all the people from the Peak and brought in the Queen Alexandra nurses. There were 3,500 people. So there they were pushed in, eight or ten to a room, men, women and children for the whole three years and eight months.

When I first came into camp, I remember being so amazed by people whom I knew very little. One person in particular brought me a candle and a flask of tea and a blanket. I didn't know her at all well but we came down to the Indian quarters and we had nothing and she came along and gave me these few things and, well, I've never forgotten. It was amazing that someone whom I didn't know very well should give me anything, because nobody gave you anything. I mean, what you had you kept, mostly. **'**

Marion Dudley was an American who was among those repatriated in 1942. She wrote a letter on board the S.S. *Gripsholm* as it was nearing New York. Possibly the wonderful sense of homecoming and liberation coloured her memories of internment. They were decidedly cheerful. Even going into the camp seemed not so bad after three weeks in a waterfront hotel.

> ‘ After the dangers of the siege and the uneasiness of the peace, it was a decided relaxation to settle down in Stanley. There was much to be done to clean up the filth and the traces of battle. But the men who had gone ahead had done yeoman service. We queued up for a meal the afternoon of our first day, which astonished us. The same ship's crew served us loyally until repatriation. It was at once evident that the men expected this to be a man's project. They completely forgot the women just as if we were so much excess baggage to be taken care of. What was our worst time? March and April, when we felt real pangs of hunger and worried over the future. The camp had been put under a Chinese superintendent and the Japanese dismissed us from their minds. The Chinese superintendent and his clan proceeded to make a good thing of us. Rations went down and down and became worse and worse. We queued up twice a day for cargo rice and thin stew which was sometimes close kin to sea water. I had some stocks of food left and was feeding all my roommates but the question was, how much to hoard for the future? Would rations stop altogether? We meticulously divided the rice almost by the grain. We ate cooked dry rice and wished for more. Tiny half slices of bread came from town spasmodically, sometimes whiskered with mould. Fortunately, my stock of coffee lasted out the six months — not so sugar, milk, butter or jam. Sweets and fats we craved most of all. During this time we were cut off completely from all communication with town or with our Japanese conquerors. ’

The camp was not put under military discipline until 1944. One of the early Japanese commandants was Yamashita, formerly a barber at Hong Kong's leading hotel. It was up to this ill-assorted medley of people to sort things out for themselves. The Americans were less rigid than the British and quickly organized themselves. John Stericker was camp secretary for the British internees.

‘Awful things went on really, I mean, I should know, I was administrative secretary of the camp and on the committee. The committee met twice a week, I suppose. Yes, I think one found out suddenly that those one would think of in ordinary civil life as the nicest people, turned out to be the worst and vice versa. It wasn't a continual case of rowing, it was very largely nerves. If you have to sleep eight or ten in a room for three years and eight months and you're terribly lacking in food, you tend to be irritated much more easily than you would be in normal life. I wouldn't say they actually rowed to that extent.’

The fundamental necessities of life were the chief preoccupations of the inmates. Food, first and foremost, and to a lesser degree, clothing. There was queuing at the cookhouse and enforced rationing — this was where you looked over your neighbour's shoulder and counted how many pieces of meat were on his plate. Jean Gittins remembers to this day this kind of meanness.

‘The ration lorry came in each morning. Our Colonial Veterinary Surgeon waited in attendance to inspect and, if considered necessary, to reject as inedible the meat provided. When this happened, internees did without. Only once do I recall having tinned herring as a substitute. It was when I was still in the married quarters. There were nine, including four babies, in our room to share the solitary tin of herrings provided. I was out when it was issued and I remember feeling quite pleased on my return to see half a fish on my plate instead of the usual stew. "You should have had more than that," my friend whispered, "there were seven herrings in the tin and only nine of us." On enquiring, I found that even though her child was too young to eat its share of fish, its mother, who had collected the tin and made the division, had kept almost two whole herrings for herself. That even she was ashamed was quite obvious: another bit was hastily added to my plate. What a thing to argue about! 0.28 part of the one herring.’

‘Andrea’ (Dorothy Jenner), a journalist and an actress in the Hollywood of the 1920s, was a down-to-earth Australian who went around ruffling quite a few feathers of camp dignitaries on the subject of food. But she had to admit that men, as cooks, were fairer.

> ❛ The food we got was hardly enough to keep a mouse alive so we were all gradually wasting away. Every day we'd stand in a queue for our tiny bowl of rice and a few garlic tops which looked like tired kelp. Garlic clears the intestines like nothing else in the world and as everybody else was eating it too the bad breath didn't matter. The garlic came in great truckloads and groups of men were detailed to boil this and the rice and then distribute it equally around the inmates. Sometimes there was a bit of meat too which they also had to hand out. The cooks were rostered: one week one lot and the next week another lot. One day one of the women came to me and said that she'd seen one of the men on cook detail snitch a bit of meat and tuck it down his shirt. Feelings ran very high. We called a meeting and used every bit of bad language you've ever heard. We abused the men tooth and nail and then voted them out and the women in. I wasn't going to be a cook but one of the women who had owned a restaurant in Hong Kong was, along with the Chinese prostitute from our block and a couple of others. What d'ya know? Within a couple of weeks these women were bigger thieves than the men and we had to get them out and the men back. ❜

She managed to get some booze to help forget life's rigours.

> ❛ Quite a lot of people had friends who sent in food parcels and sometimes they would sell you a bit of something against an I.O.U., redeemable at some unspecified future date. I never received a food parcel, but I did better than that. I got a present of a whole bottle of sherry from one of the Japs at headquarters. What brought on this sudden burst of generosity I cannot imagine, except that perhaps he'd tried out other similarly labelled bottles and found them so unpalatable that there was no anguish in giving it away. The fellow who gave it to me was a Japanese born in Hong Kong. From time to time he gave me small gifts wrapped in Japanese newspaper. I always passed this paper on to the few people in the camp who could

37

read Japanese and in that way we learnt a little about what was going on outside. This particular day the Japanese fellow gave me the bottle of sherry and said, "You have this, it will do you good." If I had shared it around all the people in the married quarters, we'd have ended up with half an eye-dropper full each. So instead I shut myself in the "john" and drank the whole bottle on my own. I knew it was selfish but I did it anyway. I wiped myself out and came out yelling "Where's the bloody Japs, let me get at them!" '

The veneer of civilized behaviour was very, very thin. There was a blackmarket where exorbitant prices were charged. With it there was thieving. According to John Stericker, it was the police who were the ring-leaders here.

' What really saved our lives was the most extraordinary thing of the whole camp. We had one or two Europeans, very respectful Europeans who spoke Japanese. They'd lived in Japan and they got to know the Formosan guards who were all for making a bit of money and as we had a lot of women in the camp, they had diamond rings or wedding rings, which were never taken from them. People had various valuables — I had some very nice gold links and studs which were given to me for my twenty-first birthday. The guards began buying this gold through our Japanese-speaking Europeans at fantastic prices. Some people had millions of yen but that didn't buy very much because equally the Formosans, who brought in food from outside, had paid thousands of yen for it. I mean, I actually spent £500 for what would have been £25 worth of food at pre-war prices. '

Jean Gittins tells of the raids on the food godowns:

' When the police were up at St Stephen's College there was nothing for them to do. They loafed around, swore at one another or just sat and stared at the godowns opposite. Remember, the rank and file of the force consisted of young men, many of them drawn from the slums of Glasgow, Liverpool or the Tyneside. Imagine how they must have felt — tons of food which rightfully belonged to us and all

38

they could do was think about it. This made them hungrier still. Someone told me that some of them began scouting around at night and soon devised a scheme to raid the stores. Comparatively little was taken to begin with, mainly tinned stuff like corned beef, soups and butter from Australia. They gorged themselves and buried the rest on the hillsides. It happened that one of them managed to sell a tin one day, and another, and they realized what a fortune could be made by exploiting fellow internees. It was impossible to conceal their sudden affluence. Their movements were watched and the rest of the block joined in the raid. **'**

Some of this food was sold on the blackmarket.

' In the queue one day the subject of our discussions centred around rising costs in the canteen. I mentioned that during my first week in camp I had met a young man one evening — one of our own internees — who tried to sell me a tin of golden syrup. He wanted HK$12. Hong Kong currency was still being used and had not been devalued. He had also a small packet of Australian cheddar which he said was a bargain at $8. The normal cost of these commodities at that time was about $1 and 60 cents respectively. I thought the prices were exorbitant and told him so but I regretted not having taken advantage of his offer because such things were no longer available at whatever cost. Even the most inferior type of slab sugar, commonly known as "wong tong" and the only sugar available, was being sold at the canteen for twice the price of the syrup. **'**

In the end nobody gained from this illicit venture.

' One fine morning rice grains on the road aroused suspicion. The trail led to our police block. Before the search party reached it the police internees began frantically throwing their loot into the bushes. What they couldn't hide they flushed down the lavatories. It was a wicked thing to do when so many were starving and the food could have been shared by the whole camp but the culprits could not afford to be caught. People do strange things under strange circumstances. Had our own representative known about it, an approach might have been made to the Japanese to release the supplies for the camp but, in all probability, the request would have been turned down. The culprits were punished of course. They were given half rations for a week and the entire block was restricted until they were transferred to the newly repaired Indian block. It could have been worse. **'**

It could have been worse. The phrase must have summed up for many their assessment of this experience. But there were compensations — time to think, to study, and to play. One internee, then a child, still thinks that Stanley was a marvellous place to grow up, almost one big happy family, so many aunts and uncles and no school. In fact, there were schools and exams and many other organized activities, which kept minds active and bodies alive. Even the grim day-to-day existence did not seem so intolerable if people kept their sense of humour. On the subject of 'night frequency' Dorothy Jenner describes one of her amusing experiences:

' There were several vegetable gardens being tended by various groups of prisoners. The fellow who had been the head of the Hong Kong Customs led a band of men in trying to cultivate one of these plots and it had a very funny story attached to it. I was becoming more and more embarrassed by the comments made by everyone in my quarters when I used my IXL jam tin during the night. So I decided to have another scout around the tracks and see what I could come up with. I found the most magnificent earthenware pickle jar. I thought that this would be a quieter receptacle than the tin, but there was a problem because the pickle jar had a very narrow neck and I wondered how I was going to get what was inside me inside it. Well, practice makes perfect, so I decided to practice and after a while the story went about the camp that Jenner was a very straight shooter. Then one day I received a visit from the head of customs who was a "frightfully nice Englishman with a lot of teeth". He asked if he could have a word with me in private. I said "Certainly", which meant of course everyone else in the room was agog to find out what was so personal that it had to be said in private. We went out into the corridor and the minister hemmed and hawed quite a bit before he said the chaps in his billet were trying to grow a vegetable garden. I said, "Oh, how wonderful." Then he hemmed and hawed some more and eventually he said, "And we've heard that you have a 'night-time frequency' so we wondered whether we could come to some arrangement. We'd like to propose that we'd give you four tomatoes a week if you would give us your morning pickle jar." Poor man, he was terribly embarrassed. But I was so thrilled at the prospect of the tomatoes and of being some use that I wasn't in the least put out and the deal was clinched. Every morning I'd go down to their quarters with my pickle jar and later in the day one of the men would return it to me. The story soon got out and the rest of them would make jokes about Jenner's pickle jar run, but I didn't mind and I had my four tomatoes. It got to the point where if I'd had a quiet night and had nothing to give them I felt quite guilty. I helped fertilize their garden for some long time until they had to give up gardening because they became thinner and thinner and didn't have the energy to do it any longer.'

And how much did starvation reduce people's sexual drive? This is 'Andrea's answer to that question:

' As far as I was concerned I became a nun, and for the entire three and a half years I was in that camp I remained celibate. Even though this was very much against my real nature, I made a pact with myself that I'd never get into a position were I could be discovered by a Japanese guard in an embarrassing situation. This decision had a lot to do with personal honour and also with the honour of my country. I wouldn't give a Jap soldier the pleasure of being able to snigger at me and, through me, my country. It's funny but it was a very strong feeling with me. There was no way in these circumstances that sex could be the beautiful, private thing that it should be. It became a mere animal act. A quick copulation in the bushes or an empty grave or in a tiny broom closet. No thank you, not for me. But you were forever seeing couples disappearing into graves and popping out a quarter of an hour later. Other favourite spots were broom closets and the flat roofs of our billets. The Japanese could watch all these goings on through field glasses from their headquarters. Eventually they sent down an edict saying that married couples must no longer use the roofs to have sex and added in Japanese — bad English, 'only good friends'. Well you nearly got knocked down for the rush of good friends!❜

The merry-go-round of life in Stanley slowly revolved but, in 1942, there was one excitement when the showground animals came to life. The drama was front page news in the English newspaper, the *Hong Kong News*, published by the Japanese and distributed to the internees.

❛ Fierce tiger shot in Stanley woods!
Successful Hong Kong police hunt in early morning!
Although, for some years past, rumours had circulated that there were tigers roaming the Hong Kong hills, it was not until yesterday morning that such was proved to be fact and the feat of shooting the first tiger on the island was accomplished by Nipponese gendarmes and Indian and Chinese police at the back of Stanley village. Early yesterday morning the lowing of wild beasts was heard by many residents in Stanley village and gendarmes and police and military set off fully armed, to search the hills. The search party, consisting of Nipponese gendarmes and Indian and Chinese policemen, was headed by Lt Colonel Hirabayashi. The party was divided into smaller groups and a net was spread around the woods. After going over the ground, for some considerable time, one group of searchers came across the tiger's lair. They immediately opened fire but despite all efforts and the use of big wire netting the beast succeeded in evading the hunters. Not discouraged by the failure of the first attempt, the Nipponese police continued their search and a bigger cordon was thrown around the whole area.
Apparently alarmed by the noise the tiger rushed about the forest for some time when it was again encountered by the police party. The police opened fire and shots from an Indian policeman this time found their mark, causing the tiger to halt. The Indian fired three shots, hitting the tiger in the head, left shoulder and lungs.❜

The Japanese didn't let this opportunity go by to drive home a propaganda point about the future of Hong Kong.

> ❛A party of pressmen, invited to Stanley to see the tiger yesterday morning, found it weighed about 240 lbs. and measured 3 ft. high, 73 inches long, with a tail of 90 inches. According to the Chinese, the appearance of a tiger is an omen of the approach of a period of prosperity.❜

One thing to be sure, though, the three thousand-odd inhabitants of Stanley Camp had one thought on their minds, more deep-rooted than the desire to be rich. That was to survive!

4 Life in Stanley Camp

Professor William Sewell had been a teacher in Chengtu University. He and his family were Quakers and they were predisposed to see the best side of people's behaviour to each other. Before going into Stanley, the Sewell family camped out in a war-damaged mansion on the Peak. They even managed to create a relationship of normal neighbourliness, making tea and receiving small parcels of food from the Japanese naval personnel there. This enforced toleration and appearance of friendliness stood them in good stead at Stanley.

> ‘The close intimacy was something that affected us all. We could never escape from each other. In our tiny room one wet afternoon, eight-year-old Ethel Dale, who was fair like her mother, and Guy were playing with a toy train which had been found in the camp. Backwards and forwards the engine ran over the line, from below the window under the table and round to the door. Joy was sitting on her bed with Joan Corona from the kitchen, sewing dolls' clothes from bits they's found in a dustbin. They were using, as thread, some fine strands unpicked from lamp wick the welfare had given them. Vee was up on the day bed reading a story. Mary, having borrowed Gladys's electric iron, was pressing the clothes and hanging them up on the mosquito net wires. They were what Guy called "dark white" but, with only cold water and practically no soap, washing wasn't what it should be. Between the wardrobe and the fireplace was our kitchen, a tin still half full of hard tack which the Japanese Major had given us, on which our electric hot-plate was set. I was sitting by this on a soap box, stirring some rice gruel and trying to read. The whole thing was fantastic and yet it was normal, except that in good weather, unless it was too hot, the children could play on the roads and hill-sides and I could sit in the shade of a chimney-stack on the flat roof for quiet study.’

However, as Professor Sewell was to write in his book of impressions about life in Stanley, *Strange Harmony*, they had to tread warily among the spikes of self-interest in this nearly egalitarian society.

> ❝In our democracy, where all were equal, it was frequently difficult
> to get things accomplished. When people were hungry, their sense
> of humour was lessened. Offence was easily given and irritation was
> quickly aroused by the shortcomings of others, as one of the men
> said about his four room-mates. "If they think I'm ordering, or am
> superior in any way, the whole lot of them will become unco-
> operative," We had to discover a middle path between an unplea-
> sant critical attitude to unsocial neighbours and being trodden
> under foot.❞

He describes how there was little privacy:

> ❝In the ordinary life of the world, people either rarely see their
> neighbours or else meet them out of doors in the street, neatly tidied
> and dressed, their minds never off guard. We knew each other so
> well that nothing was hidden. Everyone knew how we behaved in the
> bathroom and at the sink. Normally it's a problem how to foster
> fellowship among comparative strangers. With us, it was how to live
> happily with people we knew only too well.❞

At times there were grievous disputes raging in the camp. One man was
brought before an informal camp court, presided over by the interned Chief
Justice, Sir Athol MacGregor, for allegedly misappropriating communal wood
earmarked for making coffins. The repatriation issue, whether or not the
British might be allowed to follow their American cousins to their native land
in exchange for Japanese interned in Britain, simmered on for years.

Stanley camp had a theme song, *Sail Away*:

> ❝We're going to sail away,
> We hope internment here will end some day
> We want to go,
> Though we've got no dough
> Yet we're yearning to see the land that we love so
> We're going to sail away, sail away

And that day when this camp embarks
There'll be happy hearts and free
When we're putting out to sea
Afloat on a boat, on the way to Lourenço Marques.'

Even the receipt of food parcels produced wrangles as to how they should be shared out. Jean Gittins, a Eurasian, recalls the ill-feeling and tensions:

' There were some Britishers who felt that if it was not for the many Eurasions in the camp, there would be sufficient food for them. Racial discrimination had by no means moderated in the face of general adversity and that type of person was too bigotted in outlook to understand that the food was provided, not in a lump quantity, but rationed by the Japanese, according to the number of mouths to be fed. Then there were those who failed to get parcels becoming increasingly jealous of those who did. They were envious, not only of the large business houses whose parcels came regularly and had to be paid for at the end of the war, but also resentful of the fact that the Eurasian community had relatives in town who sent parcels from sheer solicitude, often at much personal sacrifice. One of our neighbours worked himself into a bad humour on each parcel day. He repeatedly advocated the pooling of all parcels, even though less than 10% of internees received them, suggesting that the contents by divided equally between three thousand others. It is interesting to note that the same gentleman and his wife, living on bare rations, became pitifully emaciated, so that they had to draw regular extras from the health clinic. Whenever vitamins became available, they were among the first to get them. We were all stunned to find at the end of internment that, instead of eating the contents of their comfort parcels from the Red Cross, they had saved intact at least one parcel each, besides tins of corned beef, presumably for a rainy day.'

Of course there were a few breaks in the tedium of this thread-bare existence. The celebration of Christmas, for instance, once again sensitively described here by Professor Sewell:

❛Christmas in 1944 was one of valiant effort. Apart from the usual monthly canteen, when we could each purchase one pound of brown sugar slabs and half a pound of egg yolk for 55 yen, there was a special Christmas canteen. We were excited to see the samples on show in the window. On rough Chinese paper were set out the dark coloured noodles, a small mound of rather dirty, ground rice and some rice-flour cakes. There were two piles of strangely coloured boiled sweets deliquescing in the humid air. Some flies lazily buzzed around a bottle of sugar water labelled "syrup". To make it all the more pathetic, on a box in the centre was a small bunch of yellow chrysanthemums. For our family quota we spent nearly 270 yen or nearly £15 sterling at the current camp rates, although all we obtained was a handful of carbohydrates. They provided variety and change for our Christmas fare. The real Christmas spirit was there however. A special effort was made by the community to bake our individual cakes made of rice and bean-flour and bran. We sat in the pitch darkness, in the biting cold wind outside the bakehouse, waiting for the ovens to be opened. A bunch of young girls started humming carols and soon we were all singing softly, carried along by the stream of goodwill that flowed down through the ages. From its last remaining stocks, the camp also gave each of us a small loaf of real bread. The flour was pre-war and decidedly musty. Even the weevils in it had died of malnutrition, yet it tasted to us as good and as rich as plum pudding.❜

There was a touching exchange of gifts in this Stanley family.

❛Joy gave to Vee a yeast pill wrapped in blue paper, a gift just as costly as the widow's mites. She gave me three pieces of notepaper for sermons and lectures, while from Vee came five sweets. From Guy a small piece of blackboard chalk which he had found. The children received a haversack each made by Mary and some friends from the unwearable Red Cross shorts and shirts and so we were prepared for the day of our release.❜

Somehow, too, the fathers of the interned children, themselves prisoners in

Shamshuipo, managed to arrange for a small present of sweets to be given to their children in Stanley.

> ‘ The prisoners of war left in the Shamshuipo camp sent, through the local Red Cross, money to buy about seven sweets each for the camp children. This gift, to celebrate the birthday of the Babe, raised up our spirit with great joy. A thought like this for the children was different from the usual attitude of most of our camp. "But you must remember," said Elma Dale, "that the least selfish of Hong Kong's men are not civilians, but prisoners of war." ’

This note of normality was rare. Alas, in this cabinned, crippled, confined captivity, there was much evidence of mental unbalance. The politics became very Byzantine. The Colonial Secretary, Franklin Gimson, an old school administrator, was determined to keep the British flag flying and was hated by a lot of internees for sacrificing their right to be removed from this place. Some of them thought they were being allowed to remain prisoners so that, at the end of the war, Hong Kong would still be a British colony. Poor Gimson saw conspiracies everywhere. Once the Vice-Chancellor of the Hong Kong University was suspected of attacking the Colonial Secretary in a lecture on Wordsworth. And this is what Gimson confided to his diary about a camp entertainment:

> ‘ *Friday, 12th March, 1943.*
> I saw a performance of the *White Cliffs of Dover* which was certainly being played to enthusiastic audiences. The production is certainly artistic, but I feel myself that its appeal to camp audiences is only of sentimental value and does not bring out the true spirit of loyalty. True loyalty is, in my opinion, not confined to lip service but the manifestation of a spirit of obedience and acceptance of sacrifice. ’

Life was not always so serious. The camp, like the military POW camp at Shamshuipo, had its concerts and other entertainments. Local music teacher, Betty Drown, played one of the two battered pianos which did valiant service and composed the camp theme song. The inimitable 'Andrea' produced several plays, among them Noel Coward's *Private Lives.*

❛ One day after we'd been in camp for a couple of years, someone said what a terrible pity it was that we couldn't put on a play of some sort. Immediately I thought of my book and said, "Why can't we? I have a collection of Noel Coward plays." I told them that I could produce a play — never having done so in my life, but never mind about that, I was sure I could, and I did.

First of all I held auditions and chose my cast — just four people. There was a young English couple, Mr and Mrs Mills, who were both natural actors. He'd worked for the Hongkong & Shanghai Bank. What a waste! The other couple were a half-Ceylonese chap, Hans Lorenz, and his English wife — such a mixture. We rehearsed like mad out in the grounds, always accompanied by a Jap soldier who hung around with his bayonet at the ready to make sure we didn't try to get up to no good. We had to ask permission from the Japanese hierarchy in town to put the play on and I was so amused, when we got permission back, to see that they'd only made one slight alteration to the text. There is one line which reads: "China very big, Japan very small." They changed this to read: "China very small, Japan very big." The play became a focal point for the camp, so that by the time we got to dress rehearsals, people came forward with everything we needed. Some of the residents of Hong Kong had actually brought evening dresses with them so we managed to assemble a terrific wardrobe for the two married couples in the play. The women were beautifully made up. We were never short of lip rouge — I think there was enough lip rouge in the camp to paint the whole of mainland China red. An English nurse was in charge of set decoration. We had to have the stage made up as two separate apartments and she did a really fabulous job. On the opening night, the Japanese all came out from town with their ladies to sit in the front row. I suppose they were going to be quite sure that they heard that magic line: "China very small, Japan very big." They didn't say anything after the performance, but they must have enjoyed it because they came back on the next night to see it again. We ran it for a week and after that we did *Springtime for Henry*. ❜

There was no lack of time to do the things impossible in normal life. Sub-Lieutenant Bush, a sailor, should not have been in Stanley. He should have been experiencing the military rigours at Shamshuipo. But the Japanese remembered his wife who was a Japanese herself and so, for about a year, until she was shipped back to her homeland, he was able to enjoy the civilian academy at Stanley.

    ‘ There was no lack of teachers and regular courses were established in literature, commerce, medicine, philosophy and nursing. There was also a school which provided for primary and higher education and examinations were held, even for University degrees. I boiled rice, dug graves, studied the stars, learnt how to lay bricks. I read quantities of bad poetry, I listened to concerts, I tried to teach certain interested people the elements of intricate Japanese language. One morning in April 1943, I was told to pack my kit. At the camp office a host of friends saw me off in a car escorted by a Japanes major. I was sorry in many ways to leave the many good friends I'd made in Stanley but I felt that now at last I should be taken to join my comrades and looked forward with much anticipation to hearing how they had fared and to being able to relay the tidings from Stanley to husbands, fathers, brothers, sweethearts and friends. I shook hands with Nakasawa and the former Hong Kong barber Yamashita. I believed they'd always tried hard in the interests of the internees and did so under extremely difficult conditions. ’

So far as the experience of Japanese camps goes, life in Stanley was not all that bad, despite the toll of life-long illnesses, particularly beriberi, caused by the deficiencies of a meagre diet. The death rate was much lower than in other camps in Japanese-held territories. Even lack of clothing meant that bodies were exposed to the sea and the sun, which the captors could not deny. At the end of the war the camp children may have had the acquisitive instincts of Fagan's urchins, but they looked bonny. Today it's all a memory. The boy who went around searching for regimental cap badges lying on the ground, tokens of desperation and defeat, is a friendly, relaxed top executive in one of the estate companies which have flourished in the booming redevelopment of Hong Kong after the war.

❟ We used to go to school in the morning — I was only seven at the time when we went into camp and the younger children went to school in the morning, the older ones in the afternoon. Quite often when we were heading up to St Stephen's College where the school lessons took place, we used to look for live bullets on the way. We used to hammer the heads off the cartridge. Apart from looking for live bullets we used to collect the cap badges of any of the regiments that fought in Hong Kong. Quite often, as you can imagine, we didn't even get to school. A few of the other things we used to do: we used to go around behind St Stephen's and try and trap birds, usually sparrows, sometimes even pigeons. We used five house bricks — four forming the base and then one balancing on two little twigs with a piece of string attached — and quite often we used to catch birds. We'd take them home to my mother and ask her whether she'd cook them. She'd take one look at the sparrows and say, "By the time I've finished taking the feathers off that, there will be nothing left." So she wasn't very interested in cooking our birds. One of the other things we did earlier on in the camp, afte a typhoon: we were allowed to go down to Tweed Bay to swim. We had a long walk by the side of the prison. Whenever there was a typhoon, there was always a bunch of kids trying to get down to the beach first to see whether there was any driftwood to carry back for cooking purposes. Because we were nearer the end of camp, we all dug up the floor boards. These were the parquet floor boards, with tar under the bottom, so they lasted a very long time and they were excellent for cooking. ❟

There was one common denominator — this three-year eight-month hiatus in people's lives. But everyone's experience was different. The following are the collected impressions of a mere handful of those thousands of internees:

❟ I was born in Stanley Camp and naturally my memory of the camp is rather hazy. At one point we were told we had to bow every time we met a sentry or the guards, we had to bow low, but they also had to bow low to us. So a whole lot of the little children went along and they kept passing the sentries, bowing to them and the sentries had

51

to bow back to them. So for a little while this game went on until it was stopped. I remember a lovely scene one day of a Formosan guard going along with his bandy legs and a line of little boys all with their sticks over their shoulders, walking along with bandy legs behind him.

I emerged, I think, with a better understanding of people and certainly a great deal more sympathy for the people we now call under-privileged.

We organized examinations, School Certificate and Matriculation examinations and submitted the papers to London at the end of the war and they were recognized by London University.

One of the things we certainly learnt in camp was the value of having a mind that you could keep active. It didn't matter what you turned to — it might be double entry book-keeping or it might be trying to learn architecture when you weren't an architect at all. Foreign languages, engineering, writing books or poems, new languages, anything — keep active and it made a tremendous difference.

People that you'd have thought would have been Christian were not and the ones who didn't profess to be were so good and kind.

Many wanted to get together in the camp — we always said, "Well, we'll meet you at the graveyard." It sounded actually very funny but to us it was a wonderful spot. It was very peaceful there — you know, the old trees and all the old grave stones and we used to read the names and think back over the people who first came to Hong Kong and specially about a lot of children's graves there. We used to wonder what they looked like and what they were like. Then we could look out at the sea and we used to stare and stare and we imagined we used to see ships coming in — of course they never did come but it was just a make-believe story.

At the time it seemed a terrible waste of a long period of one's life but in many ways it was a very interesting experience, it was rather like being a child again. There were very few responsibilities and there was very little one could do to shape one's life. There was lots of time to think — time to read. I think that I found time to think more, to read more, to take part in more serious discussions than ever I do normally. We had our moments of depression when fellow internees were executed for having radio sets or when a bomb fell on part of the camp and fourteen people were killed, when the news was bad or when rations were reduced, but generally speaking we were very optimistic. We were busy with our jobs, there were church services, lectures, concerts, ballets, plays, swimming. After the fall of Germany our hopes rose pretty steadily and we were prepared for a very long and weary wait. The end came very much sooner than we had expected. 〉

Even during the seemingly endless days of internment unexpected small things happened to cheer up the inmates of Stanley and give them hope:

〈 In our camp, there was only a bit of beating up. You never quite knew how the Japanese were going to react. I can remember coming down from the Japanese headquarters, which was on a bit of a hill, and as I came down the hill there was a Japanese NCO outside the gaols. He was obviously the driver of a Japanese officer who had gone into the gaol and he called me over. I thought I was going to be smacked because they loved smacking people, so I bowed to him — we had been told we had to bow to them. To my surprise he took a bottle of Pascall's barley sugar drops out of the back of the car and emptied them into my pocket. So he said "You!", and then sort of waved his hands for me to go away and those sort of unexpected things happened. Colonel Hatori was our camp commandant. He was 6 ft. 3 ins. I think he had been Consul General in Melbourne for the Japs. He told Sir Franklin and myself not to worry, we were bound to win the war. And then, when reports of our camp being very bad got out, the Japanese cleaned up the camp a bit and sent in eight Japanese news reporters to see our camp. Now we had not only the *South China Morning Post* reporters but some international reporters as well, so they were told to take the Japanese reporters round the camp. Afterwards I asked one of these people "What did they say?" "Oh," he said, "they were priceless, they kept on telling us not to worry" — this was about 1943, long before the war ended —

"You're bound to win this war, everything is going fine for you." That was actually in the middle of the war, in the middle of our camp, being told by the Japanese not to worry. **,**

The Stanley Internment Camp
(VII-XIV)

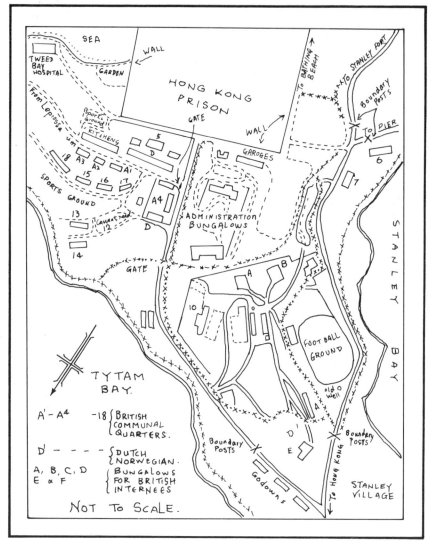

VII. The European population of Hong Kong was removed to the Stanley Peninsula on the south side of Hong Kong Island. The internees, guarded mainly by Korean auxiliaries, were not, until 1944, regarded as prisoners-of-war. They were housed in school buildings and the houses and outbuildings attached to Stanley Gaol and interned for their own protection — according to the Japanese version of events. Also, of course, it was necessary for the occupying forces to attempt to isolate these enemy civilians from the local population.

This map shows the geography of the camp and it was drawn after the repatriation of the United States civilians, who were also interned in January 1942. (*A. Birch*)

"MEMORIES" of STANLEY
1942.

VIII. As in the military camps. across the harbour in Kowloon. the traumatic experiences of this upheaval in peoples' lives, where rich and poor, important and insignificant were reduced to the common denominator of being bodies with rumbling, ever unsatisfied stomachs, brought out hitherto unknown qualities in these people. This sketch by a fortunate American shows only some of the less pleasant aspects of Stanley life. (Á. Birch)

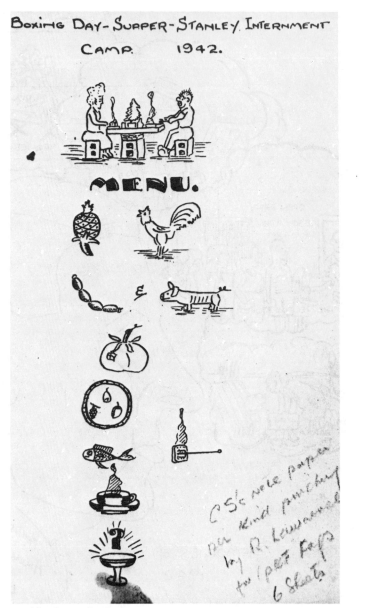

IX. A cryptic menu celebrating Boxing Day Supper, December 1942. A further sidelight on the way in which the internees obtained some of the necessities of life is indicated in the note on the corner of this piece of paper. It reads: "C. [olonial] S's [Secretary's] paper per kind pinching of R. Lawrence for One packet Fags [Cigarettes] Six Sheets."

(A. Birch)

It is with the utmost regret that I have to report that the death of Sir Vandeleur Grayburn occurred at 7.30 a.m. on the 22nd instant in the Stanley Prison Hospital. The funeral procession will leave the mortuary at the Tweed Bay Hospital at 6.15 p.m. and the funeral will take place at the Stanley Cemetery at 6.30 p.m.

Camp Commandant.

23rd August, 1943.

X. The two stark illustrations (X and XI) tell a story more directly and more tragically than any number of words.

Sir Vandeleur Grayburn as Head of the Hongkong and Shanghai Bank in Hong Kong was arrested, imprisoned and tortured in the Prison building at Stanley. He was suspected of being leader of an espionage ring responsible for smuggling British Army Aid Group intelligence messages and money into the Camp. This brief announcement, signed by the ex-Colonial Secretary, Franklin Gimson, had to remain silent on these tragic events. (*A. Birch*)

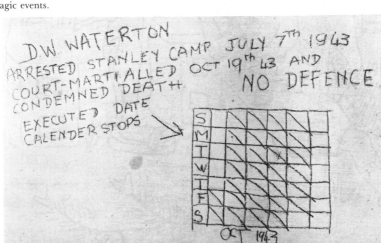

XI. D.W. Waterton was one of seven unfortunates, including, J.A. Fraser, the former Defence Secretary who were executed on the beach at Stanley by the Japanese for their involvement in operating a secret radio set in the Camp.

These graffitti scratched on his cell wall in Stanley Prison mark the grim calendar of these tragic aspects of the internment. (*Imperial War Museum, London*)

XII. Evidently, as this internment sketch shows, all was not grim horror and the threat of death. Malingering or idling occurred in the labour squad when the daily chores were readily put aside for a game of cards.

(A. Birch)

XIII. Sketches of nursing in Tweed Bay Hospital, Stanley   (*Postwar miscellany by internees*)

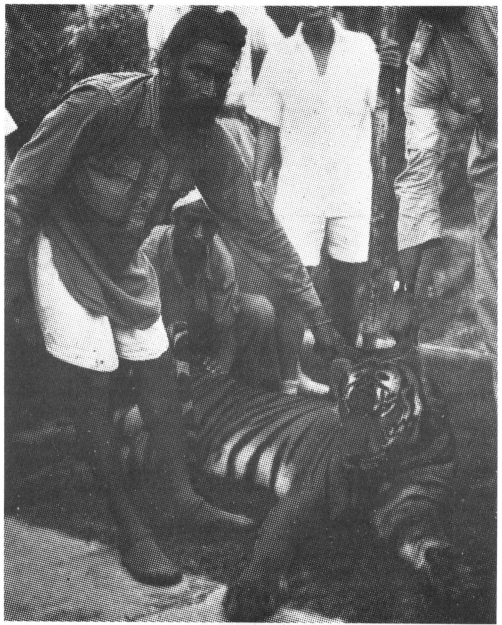

XIV. a. The famous Stanley tiger which was shot by the guards in 1942. This appears to be the only unofficial photograph taken by an internee in Stanley.

(*Lady May Ride*)

XIV. b. Skit on the tiger found in Stanley. (*A. Birch*)

5 The Prisoners of War

‘ When I consider how my life is spent,
Midst these foul buckets, I must lament
The fact that all you bastards
Need must shit
And leave the putrid stuff for me to shift,
I hope and pray you'll constipate
And stay forever in that state. ’

— poem composed in Shamshuipo Camp

For the soldier there is an easy simplicity: discipline; obedience to orders; drills; duty; death. When the order was given on Christmas Day 1941, the majority obeyed with relief. But whatever feelings of shame and surrender burned inside, there was yet another parade, to march up Nathan Road, back to their old barracks at Shamshuipo. These were now to be a prisoner of war camp. Even the commanding officer, Colonel 'Monkey' Stewart, was there to take the ceremonial salute as they marched through the gate into captivity:

‘ We were given orders to rendezvous at the married quarters along Kennedy Road. We stayed there perhaps one day, I'm not quite sure, but then we were told to be prepared to move and we had to parade at, I think, something like 4 o'clock next morning, which we did. We all paraded and we didn't know where we were going. Some of them saying we were going to be taken to Canton, others said across to Kowloon but, anyway, we were prepared for a long march. I remember putting on two pairs of woollen socks and soaping the soles of my feet, anticipating a long walk. Well, eventually we were moved out of the Kennedy Road quarters at about 5 o'clock in the morning and it was a most tedious occasion because we were told to carry our own belongings. We had duffle bags and equipment. We were marched along Kennedy Road and after about 50 yards were told to sit down and squat and then after a few minutes we were told to get up again. We were lifting our loads up and down, up and down all along Garden Road. Then we were made to sit around what is now the Chater Road Garden. At that time it was the Hong Kong Cricket Club. We were told to sit on the pavement there and then we heard martial music. We discovered that the Japanese General was coming down Des Voeux Road from west to east. The Commanding Officer was mounted and then followed by Japanese troops in a van. **9**

Captain Botelho, Commanding Officer of the Light Anti-Aircraft Company of the Hong Kong Volunteers.

6 We finally arrived at the Shamshuipo camp in the evening, I think, or afternoon, and we were told to queue up for rations. There were thousands of troops and the only rations we got, I discovered, were rice. They had the Royal Engineers in the cook house cooking rice and the queue was so long. I managed to approach the ration officer to say, "Look, you give me the rice, and we'll cook it ourselves," which he did, and being local born in Hong Kong, some of us knew how to cook rice. Those who didn't, knew how to eat the rice though. **9**

Bombardier Weller was also in Shamshuipo:

6 Shamshuipo was an absolute shambles. There was nothing there, I mean it had been completely and utterly looted. There were no windows, there were no doors and no beds; you slept on the concrete floor and there were no blankets. Morale was pretty low, I can assure you. **9**

Inevitably, there was confusion — there is one army corps that is familiarly known as the Royal Army of Organized Confusion: here it was widespread. Some prisoners, who already suffered extreme hardship at North Point Camp, were transferred to Shamshuipo. Among them was a local Chinese, a member of the St John's Ambulance Brigade, Mr Wan. He recalls:

6 Of course, there were curfews all the time. My wife often found it difficult to return to Hong Kong, so she bought a small stone hut. She could go and stay there if there was a curfew.'

The prisoners in Shamshuipo were not in the isolated confinement of the Stanley internees. Shamshuipo was a part, even than, of urban Kowloon and soldiers' wives used to visit their men to steal a glimpse or a furtive gesture of love through the barbed wire. Parcels were brought to give friends and loved ones a little comfort. However, the ordeal of these meetings was harrowing and the risks horrifying. Jean Gittins, before she went into Stanley, travelled the same wearisome road as the armies had marched to see her husband in Shamshuipo. Eventually, she was forced to give up this pilgrimage: it was too painful.

'Shamshuipo camp, where Billy was a POW, was situated across the harbour. The effort of getting there was made more arduous by a lack of road transport. What with walking between the university and the ferry and from ferry to camp and the journey in reverse we, that is, the two students and I, must have covered many miles on each visit. All this and more would have been well worth the trouble, had I succeeded in having a talk with Billy but, other than sighting him at a distance, all attempts at communication failed. We'd made three trips, spending the night before the last occasion at my sister's home in Kowloon so that we could be there early. The students had received a message from their friends in camp to say that the friendly guard would be on duty at dawn. We reached the appointed spot at 5.30 in the morning. Billy and others were behind the barbed wire fence staring into the semi-darkness, waiting. A small group of relatives, who had obviously been given a similar message, were standing on the other side of the wide road. Some of the girls sobbed quietly. The guards, they told us, had been anything but friendly, having shouted abuse at them and threatened to shoot if they moved any closer to the camp. In the murky light of early morning, we were barely able to recognize the prisoners who were dressed alike in khaki. Billy waved his forage cap incessantly. It was bitterly cold. We decided to follow the perimeter fence towards the main entrance, hoping to meet a more amiable guard.

The prisoners moved inside in the same direction without getting any closer to us. As the minutes ticked by and the the outline of the main gate rose in the distance, it began to dawn on me that our mission was about to fail. As we neared the entrance I asked the students to stay in the background whilst I went on to the little police station manned by a few guards not far from the gate. With a mixture of pidgin English, Chinese, and signs I begged to be allowed to speak to my husband. Whether these guards knew that I would be stopped by the sentries at the gate or whether they were possessed of a more humanitarian outlook I will never know, but after a short discussion, among themselves, their spokesman indicated that I could proceed. Boldly I walked towards Billy. With only a few yards between us I heard a loud commotion from behind. The guards were shouting frantically and waving their arms for me to stop. A car-load of Kempeitai, Japanese military police, had chosen that very moment to pay a surprise visit to the camp. I fled. The incident left me badly shaken and as soon as I rejoined the students, we left for home. We made our weary way in silence, lost in our own thoughts. Each visit, begun in such high hope, had in fact been nothing but a harrowing experience for, besides the frustration of fruitless endeavour, the sight of the prisoners — resembling wild animals in captivity — filled me with despair. Furthermore, I began to realize all too clearly that the danger of our being shot at was very real, whilst from the prisoners' angle our visits could be made a reason for reprisals in the camp. Above all, what useful purpose could I possibly serve by running the risk?'

Sonny Castro witnessed from inside the camp the terrible cost of these acts of love.

'Parcel day was also a gala day for it permitted a glimpse of husbands and wives, brothers and sisters, sweethearts and friends. The folks from outside would come to the camp on such a day on foot from a great distance and the prisoners of war would be clothed in their best attire, cleaner than their usual pair of tattered khaki shorts. They would try to get as close as possible to the fence wires to secure a front-row view. In order to obtain such a vantage site, the POWs would assemble hours ahead of time. It was a first-come, first-served arrangement. In the midst of silent and joyful sightings an awful scene would occasionally arise, erupting most unexpectedly. On one occasion in the early stages, on a very cold February morning, an exuberant and expectant mother called out to her husband and shouted messages to the unhappy and nervous man. She was promptly arrested by the guards and, in full view of her distraught husband and the POWs, was made to kneel, facing the fence wires. Not content with having roughly manhandled the poor woman, they tore off her dress, down to below her waist. They kicked her in the abdomen and flushed her with icy cold water all over the head and body. This went on for half an hour until she fainted and was half dragged away. The woman was never seen again after that incident and her husband went almost out of his mind. His anguish was felt and shared by all who witnessed this horrible and sadistic incident. **'**

The Japanese attitude to the prisoners was hard to understand. There were the wanton acts of brutality and capricious cruelty. Sometimes, according to the inhumanity of the individual Japanese guard or the mood of the moment, the face slapping, the killing by machine gun or bayonet might be followed by a flicker of pity. Perhaps one explanation of the general attitude was that the Japanese soldier was trained according to the harsh precepts of the Bushido warrior. The face-slapping, for instance, sometimes so vicious as to send the recipient reeling to the ground, was the accepted way of administering a reproval from the highest officer to the lowliest private. Below this hierarchy were the prisoners who had shamed themselves by surrendering. They should have forfeited their lives rather than submit to this dishonour. But what did they think of the collaborators in the camp who denounced thier comrades?

' In every community you have the good and the bad and it was no exception in Shamshuipo. We had people there who were stooges for the Japanese. I prefer not to mention their names but they made it their business to go around camp looking for information which the Japanese wanted from us, things like whether there was a radio in camp or not. I think it was largely as result of the investigations of these people that a band of Dutch submariners were caught by the Japanese with their radio and severely punished. The form of punishment was: they were made to stand on their tip-toes for 24 hours in a day and every time they lowered their heels out of fatigue they'd be beaten with a heavy Japanese military belt with a big buckle on it. But I think in fairness to the Japanese, I must say that they treated their own troops equally roughly. They were a slap-happy lot and they didn't reserve that for us alone. They were that way with their own troops. **9**

What is certain is that Chinese lives, especially those of the pitiable wretches who broke the Japanese code of behaviour, were snuffed out with a callousness which made the POWs believe that they were privileged in their treatment. An anonymous Chinese sympathizer with the captives remembers:

6 I lived opposite the barracks and I saw Japanese torture Chinese men. I think these two men went up to the barracks to steal something and they were caught by the Japanese. Their hands were tied behind them and they were beaten with sticks. They were beaten on the stomach and then, when they bent down, they were beaten on the back. Afterwards, they were tied to a pole and Alsatian dogs were set loose to bite them and then water was thrown on them. **9**

When faced with humiliations from the enemy, the soldier is trained, to a degree, to resist. The oppressions may even boost morale. However the more insidious destroyers of the will — boredom, lethargy and illness — also had to be kept at bay. Here again, the veterans of the battle for Hong Kong were perhaps more fortunate than the civilians at Stanley, who did not have the proper military discipline to support them. Sub-Lieutenant Bush wrote:

6 We were left to our own devices to organize ourselves as best we possibly could. Quite understandably, we organized the camp on a military system and it certainly worked very well, within reason that is. We didn't have very much. Whenever supplies came in, these were distributed among the various companies that were there and among the various cook-houses that were set up in different parts of the camp. It was necessary for us to stick together because we had to maintain discipline and we had to maintain morale.**'**

Bush was transferred to the camp in April 1943, by which time life in Shamshuipo had settled down into a tough routine of chores, of working parties for the Japanese outside the camp, and outwitting the guards and interpreters. He did his best to boost the morale of those who had succumbed to the rigours of this work and virtual starvation.

'The camp hospital buildings were in a shocking condition. Indeed, they were better fitted for pigs than human beings. The best that could be done was to lime-wash the walls, which produced the effect of a cattle-pen. Practically all the patients were sufferers from beriberi and particularly that form which had been christened "electric feet". A strange peculiarity of this complaint was that it was experienced only at Shamshuipo camp and not at the other camps in the area and was most perplexing to the medical authorities. Dysentery was the other terrible scourge and sufferers were segregated in a special ward. I paid my first visit to the dysentery ward to read to the patients as one of Philip Samuel's team. There were about 50 inmates, all of whom were in a serious condition. The stench was horrible; light, because of the black-out, came from low-powered bulbs shielded with cigarette tins, so that you had to sit directly below one. This provided just a circle of light on your book. It was a great strain on the eyes. The spirit of those sufferers was really wonderful. They joked about their condition — they even had bets on who would die first. None complained unreasonably and all were conscious of the fact that everything humanly possible was being done by Ashton Rhodes and his orderlies to get them well. I read them thrillers, stories by Poe, Maugham, Edgar Wallace and Wodehouse. It was really most rewarding when they laughed out loud, although this sometimes may have aggravated the conditon of their weakened bowels. But the greatest success I had was with the story, hardly appropriate in the circumstances, which I read from *Esquire* magazine entitled, "The morticians', embalmers' and funeral decorators' convention at Niagara Falls". This really had them rolling with laughter and I was implored to read it time and time again. ❯

This was a one-man entertainment, staunchly performed in the stench of sickness. But the highlights of camp life were vaudeville shows put on by Sonny Castro and his Portuguese friends.

❮ The concerts, I would say, were held maybe every three months or every six months and these were really fantastic when you consider what the members of the group had to work with as far as props and things go. Their imagination was simply fantastic when it came to making costumes and props for the stage. ❯

Sonny Castro, the star of those grim years, can still put on a performance as he recounts the excitement of the Shamshuipo hippodrome.

❮ About one hour before Curtains, the cast arrived, the female leads, barefooted and *fundosheed* (in a makeshift loincloth), carrying their own wardrobes to the wolf whistles and cat calls of the crowd. In this moment of fantastic make-believe, at times of terrible mutual adversity, it was a gala break for all, even to the Japanese sentries, who were always there, somehow back-stage, to see the women with their offers of gifts of toilet soap, sweets and cigarettes, all luxuries unobtainable for love or money in those unforgettable days. The audience could from a comfortable distance admire the stage lighting effects, settings and glamorous costumes and were, at the same time, spared the mystic odours very much on stage of saffron or curry powder, potassium permanganate, iodine, mercurochrome, sulphur and other such chemicals that went into the dyeing of the girls' costumes, home-made by camp couturiers, created from scrounged or stolen mosquito nets, tablecloths, cushion covers, pillow-cases and old curtains. The dresses and general costumery were sparkling and spanking with magnificent jewellery, the product of cut-up and snipped empty food containers for rings, earrings, necklaces, bracelets, sparkles and sequins. High-heeled shoes for the girls were made from old boots and clogs. Wigs were made from string, empty rice and flour bags. The blondes smelt worse of all, having been dyed from saffron powder. Next in line, the brunettes dyed from Chinese inks and then the red heads dyed from mercurochrome. The platinum or old women's wigs smelt best, having been caked with talcum powder. The last mentioned would invariably give off a cloud of dust and vapour when the actresses were too energetic with head movements. Thus the show of the month began, from 6.30 to 8.30 in the evening, ending with curtain after curtain call and presentations of bouquets made from grass weeds and turnip tops. To hoots and whistles, applauds and cheers, the show reluctantly came to a finale. Lights went off as suddenly as they first appeared, leaving just enough time for all to clip-clop, hobble or rush back to their huts before lights out and curfew which was 9 o'clock. **'**

In the morning after the show, there would be *tenko*, roll-call in Japanese, *Ichi, nichi, san, sei* . . . These were parades to choose drafts for transfer to Japan. Soon the prisoners would be presented with a completely different change of scene. A Lieutenant Potter was to be on that draft. Before he left Shamshuipo he wrote a poem, *Passage to the Sea*:

> In self-same manner is our life in narrow limits cast,
> In action cramped, in vision wide our mutual days are passed,
> But freedom from eternity waits through that passage to the sea.

He was to drown with the *Lisbon Maru*. For him and his comrades there could only be freedom in Eternity.

The Prisoner-of-War Camps
Shamshuipo and Argyle Street

(XV-XVII)

XV. Understandably, there were not any photographs taken with smuggled cameras or even by official Japanese war correspondents in the two camps set aside for the confinement of the other ranks and officers of the British, Canadian and Indian troops by the conquerors. However, a Polish officer of the Hong Kong Volunteer Defence Force, Lieutenant A.V. Skvorzov, imprisoned in Shamshuipo devoted some of those endless hours of captivity in making 'Chinese ink and brush sketches' of prisoner-of-war camp life in Hong Kong. These somehow miraculously survived the acute risks of destruction always imminent in the camp.

(Urban Council, City Hall Library, Hong Kong)

XV·a. Lt A.V. Skvorzov's sketches, from which a selection is taken here, demonstrate as no photographs would do, the ever-present feeling of captivity behind the coils of barbed-wire and the reduction of the prisoners to wearing the uniform of captivity, the *fundoshi*, the primitive loin cloth.

XV. b. Roll-call at Shamshuipo Camp. The prisoners were counted twice a day and several times each night.

XV. c. Argyle Street Prisoner-of-War Camp, Hong Kong.

XVI. Announcement of a Concert by prisoners at Shamshuipo, 14th November 1942. Sonny Castro was, as his racy account makes clear, one of the stars of the necessarily all-male concert parties where spirits were lifted by make-believe glamour.

There was also a sense of dry humour revealed in the playbills for these shows entertaining the prisoners and their jailers alike. This one has the pencilled approval signed by a Japanese camp official. (A. Birch)

Kai Tak Rubble Fatigue.
Nov. 1943.

XVII. Again the lighter side of the grim realities of the working parties is exhibited in this cartoon sketch by Dr Alex Mitchell. The runway of the small and primitive Kaitak aerodrome was extended by the Japanese during the occupation using the rubble of the demolished wall around the Chinese Walled City at Kowloon and the sweat of the undernourished prisoners.

(A. Birch)

6 The Lisbon Maru

‘ We were sent out in batches to do hill-cutting for expansion of the airport. That was on the Prince Edward Road side of the airport. ’

A Portuguese Volunteer

Colonel Bothelo also remembers this.

‘ Life in Shamshuipo was very difficult. In particular the period that stands out in my mind was late in '42, perhaps early '43. At that time the Japanese required us to go on working parties to Kai Tak to enlarge the airport and the daily routine was something like this. Reveille would sound at 4 o'clock in the morning. At 4.30 we'd be given breakfast, if you can call it that, which consisted of a bowl of rice and garlic water. At 5 o'clock we were put onto Star Ferry launches and taken to Kai Tak for a day's work. We'd work there until 10 o'clock in the evening and when we got back to camp, we got a meal exactly the same as breakfast. Now this would go on for thirteen days out of a fortnight and on the fourteenth day we would have a day off.

We went out on working parties. The main one was to cut down the hill of Sung Wong Toi for the preparation of what is now part of the Kai Tak airport. Cutting down a hill was a job of which few of us had any concept. We had to fill trucks with earth and then drive them down to the water front and drop them into the sea to fill in the land. The way we were cutting down this hill was very much like the seven dwarfs in the mines. While one was cutting the ground on top, the other was cutting the ground from under his feet. We had many broken arms coming back from the working parties. ’

Not only the hills of Kowloon were reduced. With pain, Sonny Castro recalls this grinding routine:

‘ The working party left camp soon after the 7 o'clock morning muster parade. It was composed of a group of several hundred men every day seven days a week and it returned to camp about 6 o'clock in the evening, with the very rare exceptions when working parties were cancelled. The men were sometimes transported by trucks and at other times by barges. Sometimes they proceeded on foot, marching whatever the distance, to the destination as dictated by the overlords. On such occasions the POWs wore what they had or what they could, in all instances torn, frayed or patched clothes. They carried their mess-tins filled with meager rations of inferior quality: cooked rice and green horrors drawn at 6.30 in the morning and eaten at noon. For footwear some had old boots, shoes or sandals, others, clogs or paper and rags wrapped to their feet, headwear, as you like it. The Japanese couldn't care less and were only interested in getting the most out of every POW, boosted by their dastardly methods of whipping, caning, slapping or rifle-butt bludgeoning of the men at work. It was common for them to pick on individuals and sometimes inflict collective punishment. They were sheer brutes. On arrival at their destination, hard labour and weather temperature permitting, the POWs stripped themselves down to their *fundoshis*, the only sensible, all-purpose Japanese piece of apparel. The men were set to work in sections, being issued with inadequate and often blunt spades, picks or shovels, baskets, poles or ropes, hammers, mallets or chisels and such other rock- and stone-breaking implements. The nature of work dictated and the area of labour indicated, away they went. To each his own, and no one with an earthly chance of doing less than his allotted share, fit or otherwise. The Japanese saw to that. The POWs had literally to cut down hills, break rocks and stones, carry rocks and sand in baskets, transfer these into wooden trolleys that ran on rails and transport the full lorries down the hill to reclaim and level areas. This done, they next shoulder-pushed the empty and heavy carts — four men to a cart — back up the hill for refilling. Two or three of the men in the party invariably suffered from acute malnutrition. If one was not working up to expectation and a little too slow for the liking of the guard, one would be buffetted and even slugged by a rifle-butt over one's shoulders and back by an irate Japanese. **,**

Then, one day, their dream of the passage to the sea came real. It was 25 September 1942. One thousand eight hundred and sixteen prisoners of war were assembled on the parade ground and were addressed by Lieutenant Hidya Wada, of the Imperial Japanese Army, through his interpreter, Nihimori Genichiro.

> ❜You are going to be taken away from Hong Kong to a beautiful country where you will be well looked after and well treated. I shall be in charge of the party. Take care of your health, remember my face. ❜

Wada's face was to be remembered. He was to go on trial for being responsible for the atrocities which followed.

The story of the *Lisbon Maru* atrocity is told from the accounts of two surviors, Geoffrey Hamilton and Alf Taylor. They are used in counterpoint, alternately: however, their common theme is one of great bravery in the face of a seemingly hopeless situation.

> ❜The Japanese sent in teams of so-called medical orderlies to test all the prospective transportees for disease before dispatch to Japan. They put their rifles down, took out white medical over-garments or gowns, put a white face-mask of gauze across their mouths and noses and with a large number of glass tubes, rather like test-tubes, they were in business. Each POW then gave his number and name, which was recorded, pasted on to a tube which was then used for the test by the POW bending down without trousers in front of the Japanese orderly who pushed it into his anus and then filed the tube. A few days later more men were called and eventually 1,809 men were recorded for transfer to Japan, including "Monkey" Stewart, the Colonel of the First Battalion of the Middlesex Regiment. Colonel Stewart, who was suffering from beriberi and the accompanying electric feet, was assigned his batman, whose sole job, it appeared, was to carry a wooden stool around so that when Colonel Stewart needed a rest, which was whenever a Japanese appeared, his orderly would set the stool down for him to sit on. The Japanese got so used to this that they took little or no notice of it.

Little did most people realize that the stool contained a wireless receiving set which was the main source of news into the camp from the B.B.C. news daily. **'**

Those clandestine contacts with the outside world, which gave hope of victory and release, were to be the cause of more blood-thirsty retributions by the Japanese later. But that is another story.

' Prisoners were loaded on 27th September into lighters from the pier at the corner of Shamshuipo camp and taken out to a freighter of some 7,000 tons — the *Lisbon Maru*, under the command of Captain Kioda Shigaru — where they were accommodated in three holds. In No. 1 hold, nearest the bows, were the Royal Navy, under the command of Lieutenant J.T. Pollock. In No. 2 hold, just in front of the bridge, were the Royal Scots, 2nd Battalion, the Middlesex Regiment, 1st Battalion and some smaller units, all under Lieutenant Colonel Stewart. In No. 3 hold, just behind the bridge, were the Royal Artillery, under Major Pitt. Conditions were very crowded indeed, with all men lying shoulder to shoulder on the floor of the hold or on platforms erected at various heights. The officers, on small twin decks, half way up the hold, were similarly crowded.

Those of us who went on board first were put into hold No. 1. These were mostly naval lads. In hold No. 2 went mostly the boys from the R.A. I went into the bottom of hold No. 2, which was pitch black and stank to high heaven, with the Middlesex, Royal Scots and other so-called small units. Once we were all on board Japanese troops, some 2,000 of them, were also loaded into the remaining holds.

The ship sailed on 27th September. The first four days were uneventful. The weather was good and the prisoners were allowed on deck in parties for fresh air and exercise. There were four life-boats and six rafts and, according to the Captain, it was decided that the four life-boats and four of the rafts should be set aside for the Japanese if required, leaving two rafts for 1,816 prisoners.

At nightfall we left Hong Kong harbour to crawl up the China coast towards Japan. All POWs were forced to stay below decks and military guards were on duty to see that this order was obeyed. One can imagine the absolute chaos and charnel-house atmosphere of each of these holds, which contained large numbers of men, with absolutely no sanitary arrangements of any sort. Most of them were suffering from bowel complaints and one of the effects of switching from a European to a rice diet was to cause one's kidneys to work overtime, processing all the water that seemed to stem from eating rice.

In No. 2 hold of the *Lisbon Maru* Lieutenant G.D. Fairbairn of the Royal Scots, Duty Officer for the day, visited the lower deck at 6.30 a.m. on 1st October to rouse the men and to ensure that they rolled up their bedding and dressed before roll-call at 7 a.m. Several of the men took the opportunity of visiting the scarce latrines on deck before the morning rush began, a wise precaution as it turned out.

On the morning of the 1st of October 1942, just about 7 a.m., a dull thud and sounds of a minor explosion shook the vessel. Nothing happened at first. Then, all of a sudden, all hell seemed to break loose. The Japanese went wild, dashing all over the place, shouting and screaming orders, bundling the POWs back down the holds, whilst the ship's crew were busy collecting the wooden plank hatch covers to place over the holds in which the POWs were housed. After the planks were put in position, tarpaulin sheets were stretched over the holds, iron holding bars inserted to keep the sheets tight and wooden wedges driven in to further tighten and secure the holds. We were really locked in. No air, no sanitation, no food, no water and no real knowledge of what had happened. Then the guns began to fire and one of the officers with us, who could speak some Japanese, picked up the word for submarine and torpedo. It seemed fairly obvious that this is what had happened. An American submarine patrolling the China coast near Shanghai had spotted us. As the *Lisbon Maru* had one gun fore and another aft the submarine had assumed that we were an armed raider. It popped a torpedo into us which hit the engine room and killed several of the duty staff there. By 7.20 a.m. the firing was over and except for a lot of running about on deck, things quietened down somewhat.

On board the ship the prisoners heard and felt an explosion, after which the engine stopped and the lights went out. But they did not know whether the ship had been torpedoed or whether there had been an internal explosion in the engine room. There was wild activity and shouting among the Japanese. Some prisoners who were on deck were hustled and pushed into holds and the ship's guns began firing. About ten sick men, who had been allowed to remain permanently on deck, were also sent into the packed holds, with an order that they should be isolated. In the holds the prisoners sat gloomily, wondering what was happening and whether they were going to get any breakfast.

On board the ship the Japanese had calmed down but were becoming uncooperative. Requests for food and water were refused. There was not latrine accommodation in the holds and many of the men were suffering from dysentery or diarrhoea. Requests for permission to attend the latrines on deck or for receptacles to be passed down were ignored. For the prisoners it was a long, uncomfortable and increasingly anxious day. It was by now clear that the ship had been disabled and was listing, but the prisoners had no means of knowing the extent of the damage or what measures would be taken for their relief.

Conditions were stifling. Many were in a complete state of apathy and just couldn't care less. Others, with more spirit, had been picking away at the hatch planks which secured us and had been making steady progress at weakening the planks with knives, pieces of iron or steel or anything that we could use to cut into wood. In the early hours of the morning of the 2nd October, the ship suddenly slid backwards into the sea. The panic was immediate and complete. Men who had been dozing peacefully one second suddenly became raving lunatics. They clawed and fought for space on the ladders down to the bottom of the hold and one of the two ladders collapsed under the weight of men crawling over each other to reach the upper section of the hold. Occasionally we could hear somebody shuffling about the deck outside and the officer who could speak some Japanese tried to make contact. The Japanese soldier outside was agreeable to talk, telling us not to worry, everything was all right.

Morale remained remarkably high. C.Q.M.S. Henderson of the Royal Scots, in particular, his beard jutting out agressively, encouraged non-swimmers like himself by insisting that now was their opportunity to learn. In the course of the long night, the men in No. 2 hold got in touch with the Royal Navy in No. 1 hold by tapping on the bulkhead, and with the Royal Artillery in No. 3 hold by word of mouth, along some sort of vent. Conditions in No. 1 hold were similar to those in No. 2 except that two diptheria patients had died. But conditions in No. 3 hold were much worse. Water was rising in the hold and the officers and men had to man the pumps. Because of extreme heat and shortage of air, men lost consciousness after undertaking a few strokes of the pump, and some of them collapsed into the water and drowned.

At some period during the night Lieutenant Colonel Stewart decided to prepare for a break-out. One of the resourceful British troops produced a long butcher's knife, which had escaped the eyes of the Japanese soldiers. Armed with this, he mounted an iron ladder, in pitch darkness, and tried to make an opening. But having to hold onto the ladder with one hand, and suffering from lack of oxygen, he was unable to effect any purchase and was obliged to abandon the attempt.

By about 9 o'clock some of the hatch planks were beginning to come apart and a little further endeavour was required to loosen them sufficiently for us to get out. Suddenly the ship rolled on its side. Another panic started with startling results. The press of men beneath the hatches was so great that the hatch covers gave way, and in a wild burst of excitement, daylight streamed in as men bundled out. The Japanese soldiers on the bridge began to shoot at the POWs who, as soon as they had collected their wits, stormed the bridge and killed them with their own rifles. A steady stream of men poured out of the hold out of which I was one of the last to leave, as I had a very sick friend who could not even get up the ladder. Eventually I got him onto deck and went looking for food and water, none of which was to be found. A broken sack of sugar lay on the deck but I was so dry I couldn't swallow it. The sunshine was magnificent, sparkling on the waves in long streams of scintillating diamonds. The fresh air and crisp Autumn sunshine, after the purgatory of the hold, made life really worth living.

The ship was still at an angle of 45°, with the bows out of the water and the afterpart of the ship disappearing beneath the sea. About half of the deck was still visible. Crowds of men were still swarming about trying to find something to eat or drink. Others were trying to launch a lifeboat which had got snarled in the falls and couldn't be loosened. Others who could swim had jumped overboard to swim to four Japanese ships which were circling us. It was obvious now that the Japs had intended that we should go down with the ship, but it was not to be. Some ten minutes later I had completed a small raft on which my two friends could sit and with our assistants we lifted the raft over the rail for a twenty foot drop into the sea, with two ropes for them to hang onto, should they part from the raft on the way down. They made it all right and the last I saw of them was both of them sitting like twin deities as the current hurried them away from the ship. The Japs were cruising around, still picking off men with their rifles. **'**

The ship, when torpedoed, had settled down on a sand bank.

' Had the ship sunk at this stage, few would have escaped, but by good fortune the stern had come to rest on a sand bank, leaving the forepart of the ship, as far as the bridge, sticking out of the water. Successive waves poured into the hold. She remained in this position for about an hour, which gave sufficient time for all live men to climb up or to be assisted out of the three holds. On arrival on deck, some men immediately plunged into the water. Others remained on deck wondering at their survival and seeking some place where they could at last respond to a long outstanding call of nature. Some men threw ropes down into the hold to increase the number of exits and Lieutenant Colonel Stewart, despite a bad leg, climbed one of the ropes and was helped onto the deck, immaculate as usual, complete with his cap and swagger cane. **'**

Alf Taylor spent the rest of that day with another POW, Private Ferris, of the Middlesex regiment, clinging to a plank in the sea.

' The ship sank, as near as I can recall, at about 9.45 a.m. on the 2nd of October, some 27 hours after the torpedo hit us. By 6 p.m. that evening, we began to draw near to land, which proved to be several islands sticking out of the sea. It was obvious that unless we wanted to be swept through the channel between the islands, we would need to start working towards the edge of the rip. This meant trying to make a landfall on the weather shore, a dangerous undertaking, but one that had to be made as there was no guarantee that if we got caught in the tide race between the islands, we would ever be able to get out of it and make a landfall on the lee shore. As we were working at this, a Chinese islander rowed from an inlet in a small sampan, came along side us and helped us into his boat. He then rowed us to shore, dumped us there, told me that there were people in the village up the hill, then dashed off to pick up some of the masses of flotsam and jetsam riding on the current. Leaving Ferris where he was, I stumbled up the hillside to a Chinese village hidden in the hilltops. My Chinese, at this time, was not very good, being merely confined to simple barrack-room Chinese, but a small boy seemed to understand what I was saying and he explained it to the men and women who were congregated there. Four of the men took a door off one of the outhouses and disappeared down the hillside to fetch Ferris. In the meantime, reaction set in and I felt completely and utterly exhausted. I asked for food and, it being meal time, I was quickly served with a large bowl of noodles and meat and all the water I wanted. They then gave me a padded quilt and guided me to the temple saying that I could sleep there on the floor. Before they left the place I was fast asleep. Next morning, at about 6 a.m., I woke and wondered where I was. The only clothing I had was a pair of khaki shorts and a pair of gym shoes. Fortunately the weather was warm. With the sun up I pushed off to look around. It was wonderful to feel free again, no Japanese, no guards, no discipline. The temple was full of men still sleeping. The outhouses were full of men, and the haystacks also. I learned later that the villagers had rescued about 300 men and fed them all as they came in one by one. With no prospects, it was decided that the only thing we could do was to send smoke signals, which the Japanese picked up. By early afternoon they arrived in some small craft to take us off the island. By this time the islanders had changed into a military type of uniform and I learned that the islands were supposed to be loyal to Wang Ching-wei the Chinese puppet governor of the Japanese. Sheer force of circumstances had dictated what the islanders had to do and, prior to the arrival of the Japanese, they were most apologetic. '

Mr Taylor survived the sinking of the *Lisbon Maru* and lived in Hong Kong until 1981 when he left on retirement. About 300 were rescued by the islanders, but the situation was not very hopeful, and in Alf Taylor's words:

' The arrival of the Japanese, who were marines by their badges, meant much shouting, jostling and confusion. One team searched all the houses, prodded bayonets into haystacks, turned the whole place inside out, rounding us up. They then escorted us to the beach where we boarded small rowing boats before being taken on the vessels in the bay. At about 5 a.m. on the morning of the 3rd of October we arrived at our destination, and were unloaded onto the quay at Soochow, some miles south of Shanghai. We were on the wharf all day and at night-time again loaded onto barges. Next day we were loaded aboard a rusty old hulk of a ship called the *Shinsi Maru*. The plate was so thin that one could poke a finger through it and the sea trickled in. This vessel pulled out from Soochow and set sail for Moji in Japan. Her top speed was four knots and she was a shocker. But at least we managed to reach Moji, where we once more disembarked to serve the rest of our time in Japan. '

Geoffrey Hamilton, the author of the second eye-witness account used to depict the events of this tragedy, also survived. He was one of the brave and fortunate thousand who were then sent to labour camps in Japan. He was to return to Hong Kong after the war to become acting Colonial Secretary. When he wrote his account of this ordeal, he noted that in an order issued in

December 1942 the Japanese army noted:

> Recently during the transportation of prisoners of war to Japan, many of them have been taken ill or have died and quite a few of them have been incapacitated for further work due to their treatment on the journey, which was at times inadequate.

In Shamshuipo the overcrowding was somewhat relieved by other drafts which found their way safely to Japan. From about 10,000 troops the number fell to around 5,000, a good number of them members of the Hong Kong Volunteers. The camp now seemed to be better organized as the local people could more easily exert their influence. Running the gauntlet of their Japanese captors, they maintained some contact with the outside world. Parcels brought relief and sometimes a glimpse of a slightly less harsh world beyond the barbed wire. They also brought love and hope. With this support to the spirit it somehow seemed easier to the prisoners to endure the rigours, to hold on and to believe in a brighter end to captivity.

Private Remedios well summed up the tenacity of the prisoners which made them hang on to survival and the hope for victory and freedom.

> ❛ "To you there can be no defeat, no failure, no loss," and as I recollected these words in the prison camp, I felt that it was indeed true; that although I'd lost everything — I'd lost my freedom, my home — yet there was a certain amount of optimism that we would triumph. We would win the war. That was something that really drove the Japanese guards very, very mad, because they could not understand how these stupid people could expect to win the war. But yet every time when they asked a British soldier, "Who do you think will win the war?", the answer was, "We will win the war!" Of course, that soldier was really stupid because he got beaten up for it. But win the war we did. ❜

7 The British Army Aid Group and Escapes

Now that the prison doors had been bolted there was at first a feeling of hopelessness. You were caught. There was not much you could do about it except to come to terms with the situation. But there were a few who realized that it would be easier to escape from captivity in the early days before the Japanese were fully in control of the camps and the Colony. Others, both civilian and military, bided their time. Conditions could only get worse. It was a question of making careful preparations and finding an opportune time. In either case, the obstacles to be overcome were great and the risks extreme. A Volunteer explains the situation:

> ❦ At the beginning of the war, the Japanese wanted to exact from us an undertaking that we would not try to escape. At first, everybody refused, because everybody considered it to be the duty of a British soldier to try and escape and rejoin his unit where possible. But General Maltby sent a message in to us to say sign it, because it's not worth the piece of paper it's written on, since it's extorted from you under duress. Most of us then signed. I say most, because there was a band of seven Irishmen, led by Bob Sheehan, I believe, who refused, who said, General Maltby, or no General Maltby, we will not sign. ❧

Colonel Ride, a doctor and a professor at the University, was a man with strong opinions about the failure of the British to put up an effective resistance against the invaders. He saw that the people of Hong Kong would need help to come through the ordeal which lay ahead. When his ambulance field unit had cleared up the battle field of the wounded and the dead as best they could, he too, was ordered into Shamshuipo camp. For him, China offered the chance to continue the fight against the Japanese. It was now or never. Colonel Ride described his plan as follows:

> ❦ For the past week I had been preparing my plans for escaping and I

told General Maltby that I was convinced that this treament by the Japanese was deliberate and I could not subscribe to the general opinion that it would improve with time. My opinion was that when the warmer weather came, it would be impossible to stop the spread of dysentery with the primitive facilities at our disposal, that the meager rice diet would so weaken the men they would fall an easy prey to any epidemic and that with summer, cholera, which was endemic in Kowloon, would certainly slay those whom dysentery had failed to kill. I was convinced that the only thing that could possibly save the lives of those 5,000 men was for someone to escape and either force the Japanese to alter their policy by pressure from without, or to smuggle vaccines and medicines back into the camp from China. I do not think either the General or the Brigadier had much faith in my plans and after some discussion I promised that I would not try to escape until I felt that all that I could possibly do in the camp as senior medical officer had been done. **'**

This was 7 January, two weeks after surrender. But as each day passed the situation became more urgent.

' Unfortunately for my promise to postpone my attempt to escape, an order to barbwire the Chinese volunteers in an isolated area of the camp compelled me to put my plans for escape into immediate action. **'**

The plan was to sneak out of the camp during the following evening to an unguarded jetty. Here, Francis Lee, his clerk at the University, would be waiting for him with a hired sampan. The route of escape would take them a short distance along the shore to a spot near the present-day San Miguel brewery. Overland they would skirt the line of hills and any Japanese patrols to the far side of the Tolo Harbour. There another junk would, if all went well, ship them to Mirs Bay, followed by a final hop to free China. Unlike Admiral Chan Chak and his large group of escapees, who left on Christmas Day and were home at Waichow in a matter of days, Ride and his university colleagues endured a journey lasting forty days before reaching Chungking, the wartime capital of China. Ride's success depended upon the resourcefulness and loyalty of a Chinese friend. Later, when Ride's British Army Aid Group was formed to help prisoners escape, things were much more organized. Runners slipped into and out of Hong Kong through the New Territories, setting up escapes. They arranged clothing, essential for disguise, and money to pay for the expenses of the escape journey. Ellen Field, a fearless worker in Dr Selwyn-Clarke's welfare organization was able to move about on the strength of her claim to Irish nationality. She tells how she decided to embark upon an even more dangerous role in helping British prisoners to get away.

❢ Late one Saturday evening in the Spring of 1942, I was relaxing after putting the children to bed when there was a faint insistent knocking on the front door. I was a little nervous and through the closed door asked: "Who is it? Who's there?" A girl's voice answered, "Alicia, it's me, Alicia." I flung the door open and saw Alicia standing there very agitated. "Is there anything wrong?" I asked in alarm. "Let me in, please, I've something to tell you," she said urgently. "Of course, do come in," I said gently. "What's the matter, what's happened, Alicia?" She broke into tears. "I've got a soldier and I've been hiding him." I looked at her in astonishment. I wanted to burst out laughing at this utter nonsense. Was she actually serious? "You've got a what?"

"My boyfriend, he didn't go to camp, he's with me. You must help him get away from Hong Kong," she pleaded. I was astounded but, at once, I desperately wanted to help this man. I would have helped the whole of Shamshuipo camp to escape if I could. All the same, if this girl was telling the truth, I was running a grave risk. The Japanese penalty for harbouring or assisting a British escapee was death. I decided immediately that this was one way to even the score against the Japanese and I remember the grinning insolent faces of 'Porky', Saito, 'Yanki' and Nomori.

"Where is he now?" I demanded. "Who is he anyway?" She said his name was Jock White, a Royal Scot, and that she had been hiding him in the back room in her servants' quarters.

"Of course I'll try to help you, Alicia. Now you go home and stay in until I contact you." Next morning, after a sleepless night, trying to think of a method of getting Jock away, I still had no definite plan. Did he just walk out? Could he be flown out? Perhaps he could go by sampan? **'**

She went to Selwyn-Clarke who, in order to protect his medical organization, refused to be involved. She was determined to do something herself, but what could she do left to her own resources? Fortunately, the British Army Aid Group decided to help her.

' For the second night I found myself unable to sleep. I tossed and turned as I tried to work this thing out. I was still wrestling with the problem late the following night when there was a soft tapping on the back door like a child's light tapping. Both Mary and I were scared, for our callers so far had always walked boldly up to the front door, and we knew there were prowlers about these nights.

"Don't open the door, Missy," warned Mary, "bad men." But the knocking was repeated, softly and insistently. I couldn't ignore it and went to the door. I opened it a fraction and peered out. There standing in front of me, only a few inches away, was the most sinister looking Chinese I'd ever seen in my life. He was very slim and dark and wore a long black Chinese gown. On his head was an ordinary English cloth cap and he had a moustache like Charlie Chan's. The total effect was enough to scare anyone but before I could get the door closed he spoke.

"Wait," he said imperiously in good English. "You have a soldier." It wasn't a question, he was making a statement. My heart almost stopped. I immediately suspected a trap. I felt sure a Japanese soldier was hidden close by waiting for a quick nod to slip forward and arrest me. I started to stammer out, "I don't know what you're talking about —, and then he interrupted me. "Don't be afraid," he said calmly. "I have come to help you."

"Who are you?" I demanded, curious now. He lifted his long gown and put his hand into the pocket of his trousers, then he brought out a well-thumbed piece of paste-board with his picture on it. There were some words written in Chinese characters and then I recognized a name in English handwriting. It was the signature of a British officer giving name and rank and it had been signed in Chungking. As though sensing I still did not quite believe in him, he said, "Whatever you decide to do will have to be done quickly, for I am now on my way back to Chungking. I have no time to lose."

"Chungking?" I queried, as though he were talking about Mars or Venus. I tried to trap him. "How can anyone manage to get up the rapids of the Yangtze without running into the Japanese?" He explained swiftly that there was a rice route leading from paddy field to paddy field, sampan to sampan, the whole way to Chungking and that it was run by guerrillas. 〉

She passed the message to Jock White, via his Eurasian girlfriend, to depart at 8 o'clock the following night. She also had to buy some items of disguise if the big red-headed Scot were to stand a chance of passing himself off as Chinese.

〈 I went then to buy what I needed at the street market just off Jordan Road. I was about to go home when I remembered the Scotsman's eyes. They were blue and would give him away completely. Frantically I looked around for a pair of smoked glasses. A man wearing dark glasses is a common sight among Chinese, as they have notoriously weak eyes, and I knew Jock would rouse no comment if he wore them. I picked up a pair and tried them on. I couldn't see a thing so I decided they would do. Back home I got through the day somehow.

As 8 o'clock got nearer, and darkness fell over the city, I kept going out on the verandah to see if there was any sign of Alicia and her boyfriend. Eventually they arrived, but Jock had hardly walked into the lighted sitting-room before I noticed his flaming hair. How had I overlooked it? I was suddenly panic-stricken but said nothing. I showed them what I had brought and fortunately the shoes and socks fitted. I'd only guessed at the size. Then Jock took off his tweed jacket and put on the cheongsam. He was an incongruous sight and said that the gown felt like an old fashioned night-shirt.

In the midst of all this there was a timid knock on the back door. Our Chinese friend was back. As he came into the middle of the room, he confronted for the first time the man he had promised to take to safety. They weighed each other up and I saw that Jock was anything but impressed. "Try the cap now," I said, anxious to see if it would hide that red mop. Jock gripped it in his two big fists and pulled it on. "Pull it further down," I urged and he gave it another tug but it was useless. I could see that alarming red hair sticking out from under it. No matter how he jammed the cap down you could still see the hair. For a moment I was almost ready to admit defeat and then I had an inspiration. "We'll dye it," I cried excitedly, and then my enthusiasm was suddenly dashed. There was nothing in the kitchen or the bathroom which would dye this man's hair black. Then, suddenly as I glanced wildly around the sitting-room I saw the writing desk and I remembered that in the top drawer there was some Indian black ink. I rushed over, pulled open the drawer and grabbed the bottle of marking ink. I held it up triumphantly and said, "Come on, I'm going to dye you." Jock looked simply flabbergasted. A first, he bluntly refused, but I was determined. I took off his cap, made him sit down, draped him with a towel and emptied the entire contents of the bottle over his head.

The Chinese kept telling us to hurry up, reminding us that they had a quota of miles to cover that night and they must manage it if the trip were to be successful. Jock put on his cap, fixed the glasses and stood up. The transformation was complete. He actually looked like a Chinese, but I warned him, "Don't open your mouth, for God's sake, or you're a dead man." "It's time to go now," said the Chinese anxiously. 〟

Then came the part Ellen hadn't bargained for. She was ordered by the Chinese runner to act as escort and decoy on the first stage of the journey, across Kowloon to Laichikok Road. The long march of Jock White had begun. Later, Ellen Field was to receive the rosary, which the young soldier said he would send her, if he got through. With it was a message:

'Thank you for safely delivering another British soldier.'

It was signed by a major from the British Military mission in Chungking.

Ellen Field was to carry out several more such missions until the organization decided it was getting too dangerous for her and for them. If she knew too much, and they were taken by the Japanese, the life-line to China would be blown. The B.A.A.G. was also in touch with the camp at Stanley, but its offer of liberty bonds was not taken up. However, in March 1942, two parties escaped from the internment camp on the same night. Perhaps it was coincidence, although at the end of the war it was disclosed, at the trial of a collaborator accused of denouncing these brave efforts, that the defence secretary, J.A. Fraser, had a hand in planning these escapes. Fraser, himself, was arrested and executed. Gwen Priestwood, together with a police superintendent and some other men, made their way to Cape Collinson, not very far from Stanley. They were then rowed across the harbour to the temple in Joss House Bay by six Shaukeiwan boatmen. From there they went west to the Sai Kung peninsula and then by the usual route to Waichow. Gwen Priestwood tells about the other party.

> ❛ Before Anthony and I escaped from Stanley word of our plans must have got around, because Epstein and his party made a break that night, some hours after the Priestwood/Bathhurst expedition got started. This party included five people, one of whom was a woman. They managed to commandeer a row-boat and, by using a blanket for a sail, were blown down the coast to Macau, a city which is nominally Portuguese territory. Here, they were not much better off because Macau was completely dominated by the Japanese. They had to re-escape again. Everyone in Camp Stanley seems to have known about the break the morning after it happened, whereas the Priestwood/Bathhurst escape did not become known until late that evening and so quite an argument raged in the camp over who got away first. I tell this small incident just to prove that ours was the first party through the barbed wire, if only by a few hours. ❜

Priestwood had brought with her the list of internees at Stanley so that the authorities at home could notify their next of kin. Surely, many plans to escape must have been laid, but luck was always a vital ingredient, as well as outside help. Whenever attempts at escape were discovered, or actual escapes carried out, the Japanese inevitably took retaliatory measures. In Stanley, the reprisals were relatively light.

‘ That night at about 9 o'clock the three chairmen discussed the matter with Mr Yamashita and Mr Nakazawa. They asked us what reasons we could advance for the escape, to which we outlined the insufferable conditions of the camp and the fact that if conditions did not improve, they could anticipate further escapes. They asked whether we would enlighten them as to the possible routes which the internees would take and we replied in the negative, pointing out that we would tell on our internees and facilitate their capture. Mr Yamashita replied that he quite understood. He stated that it was necessary for him to take some disciplinary action and he would think it over and advise us the following day.

The third day thereafter, we arrived at headquarters, accompanied by Mr Gimson. The ultimate decision on the disciplinary measures was as follows:

We would have two roll-calls on each day, one in the morning at 8 a.m. and one in the evening at 10 p.m. All lights would be extinguished by 11 p.m. All internees must be in the vicinity of their buildings at 8 p.m., Mr Yamashita indicating that, when the daylight hours became longer, he would consider application for permitting the internees to be away from their immediate buildings to a later hour. He would hold the Chairman responsible in the future, to which we replied that such responsibility could be assumed only if conditions improved. Moreover, he must realize that escape was a natural aim of every person since we were a people who loved and cherished freedom. We stated that until such time as conditions improved, we could not be held responsible, but that the best we could do would be to endeavour to co-operate in pointing out our camp deficiencies, leaving it to the Japanese to correct the situation. The room from which the American internees escaped was not to be used for billeting purposes. The camp would be patrolled at night by the gendarmerie. ’

At Shamshuipo there was a similar story. It was a cruel dilemma for the would-be escaper. For the risks to himself he alone would be responsible. There was also the knowledge, however, that success or failure would mean drastic repercussions in the camp. Some prisoners refused to contemplate the idea of freedom out of consideration for their comrades. It was to resolve this dilemma, which could be a cover for cowardice and apathy, that Colonel Ride contacted the camp, proposing a mass escape. This was vetoed by the senior officers forming the escape committee. It was left to individuals like Lieutenant Robert Goodwin, a New Zealand naval officer. His was the last escape made from Shamshuipo in 1944, and it was a triumph of determination against set-backs which would have made anyone else give up in despair. Describing his determination, a friend said Goodwin thought of nothing but escape and gave his whole time to planning it. He was like a solitary hermit, watching, planning, preparing for the right moment. He very rarely spoke of anything but escape and had very few friends. Some of the prisoners were in fact bored with Goodwin's obsession, but he didn't care what anyone thought about him. He was going. The question was: When?

Goodwin describes the first stages of his plans for escape:

‘ The discovery of the communication network and, then of the radio, caused our captors to intensify their security measures. Escape became more and more difficult. My plans were still only plans when, in May 1944, we were transferred to Shamshuipo. At first there seemed to be many obstacles to overcome but our arrival marked the begining of a train of events which eventually cleared the way for my departure. First, the concertina wire was removed from the base of the outside fence and from that moment the fence ceased to be an obstacle. Earlier inspection had revealed the place where a short section of wire mesh had been removed and at that place the lowest electric wire was high enough from the ground to allow a thin person to slide under. Next, some of the permanent sentries were replaced by a roving patrol, and an Alsatian dog took the place of one who had guarded the sea-wall beyond the electrified fence. Then a gang of men cleared the remaining petrol from the trenches and everything of value was taken from that area, including wooden bridges from the drains. The situation was rapidly developing in my favour. My spirits were leaping and my heart pounding unreasonably and I could not prevent my features from expanding in a broad grin. At that moment I knew that the time was near and there was nothing between me and the sea except two fences and the regular camp guards. Once beyond those obstacles I felt my chances of success must be good. **'**

This was Goodwin's plan:

' Careful study had convinced me that there were two possible routes out of the camp. One was by direct assault over the fences, the other was through the gate used by the sentries in passing to and from the guard house. There were serious disadvantages to both routes and at the last moment I chose the fences. Our section of the camp did not touch the sea-wall, for a hospital was situated at the north-west corner of the main enclosure. Between that hospital and our western boundary there was a vacant section on which were the concrete floors of two demolished huts. I decided to scale the fence opposite the end of that vacant section.

Let's now examine my problem in a little more detail. A concrete path ran along the northern end of the huts and outside there was a large drain 6ft wide and 4ft deep. Along the outside edge of the drain was a roll of concertina wire. Beyond that, again, there was a narrow track between the wire and the fence. Fifty yards west of my hut there was a small bridge over the drain and that was where I would cross. Along the fence, at frequent intervals, lamp posts rose three feet above the concertina wire and those were the only ones that it was possible to climb. On each alternate post there were two insulators. On one there would be bottom and third wires, on the next there would be second and top wires. I chose a post with insulators on the second and top wires. Once poised on the top insulator I'd be clear of the fatal electric wires. Beyond the main fence there was 50 yards of clear ground to cross to the second electrified fence which, as I said previously, presented no great obstacle. Then there were 100 yards of open ground to traverse to the sea-wall. Special electric cables kept the electric fence alive all night but owing to economy measures the fence lights were extinguished at mid-night. No move could be made until the lights were out so there would be, at most, six hours of darkness in which to gain distance from the camp. Once over the sea-wall it was my intention to swim across Laichikok Bay and then travel north to Mirs Bay before striking west to Waichow, on the east river. Unfortunately, except for the restricted portion, in view from the camp, the country was completely unknown to me, for by land I had never been away from the immediate vicinity of the naval yard. However, study of maps and talks with those who knew the country had given me a fair idea of the salient features of the area and, while on patrol in Mirs Bay, I had seen where the path to Waichow cut through the mountains. Waichow was chosen as the goal because some objective within a reasonable distance had to be chosen, and Waichow, being about 100 miles away, seemed to be the only logical place. **?**

Goodwin had secreted a cache of rations for the journey: a tin of corned beef, creamed rice, condensed milk, biscuits, soya bean powder and two ounces of black pepper. Other items collected for the expedition to freedom included a water bottle, two Mae Wests, a tin-opener, a pocket knife, paper and pencil, a safety razor and a spare blade. He was probably the best equipped escaper of any who went through the barbed wire. Then one night with driving rain and thunder, he carefully climbed up the insulators of the electrified camp wire, jumped and was away into the night. But even with all the planning and preparations, Goodwin ran into the most perilous situations in making his way over the hills to Shatin and then to Shataukok. The food, and eating it, became a problem.

❛ Rest was my most urgent need and after that came food. It was important to retain strength during those first days. In order to do that and, at the same time lighten my pack quickly, I had planned to use the heavy tinned foods first. For that reason, my first breakfast in freedom consisted of an 8 oz. tin of beef. The meal was far from enjoyable, for nervous tension had destroyed my appetite and each little mouthful had to be chewed slowly and swallowed with great deliberation. At every swallow I was on the verge of being sick. **❜**

Tempted just to lie down and go to sleep — and most likely to wake up a prisoner again — Goodwin resisted. But after this ordeal, there was a glimpse of freedom.

❝ Something strange was happening to my eyes and three black objects began to dance in my vision. After some difficulty in bringing them into focus I saw that they were men coming towards me. As they came closer I felt certain that they were Chinese and it was obvious that they were very interested in me. the critical moments of my escape had arrived. Were they friends? The next few minutes would decide my fate. I'd no regrets for I knew that everything possible had been done to the utmost of my powers. It was hopeless to continue alone any longer and should these men prove to be enemies, well, death would come a little sooner, that was all. I kept on walking straight towards them and they, very much on their guard, separated as I approached. Certainly my appearance can hardly have been reassuring for my shirt and shorts were in filthy tatters, while a ten-day growth of beard covered my gaunt and haggard face. We stopped and greeted one another. To come at once to the main point I stretched my hand down towards the village and said, "Any Japanese down there?" One of the men gave answer: "No Japanese, long time." ❞

Goodwin was but one of close on a thousand prisoners, internees and essential civilian workers who escaped from Hong Kong, the Captive Colony, during those years of imprisonment.

8 Those Who Stayed Out

If you had the choice, was it better to stay in town, to lead a precarious existence fending for yourself, facing the deadly and insidious Kempeitai, the Japanese secret police; or to suffer the communal rigours of the internment camps? The Japanese administration had a broad and loosely defined group, the Third Nationals — people of neutral nationality — who could not be locked up. But were they free? They'd been caught in Hong Kong during the defeat of the British. Most were opposed in spirit to the conquerors. Some could take advantage of the Japanese inducements to leave Hong Kong for the little treaty port of Kwongchouwan, west of Macau. But others stayed to look after their property. There were some like E.J. Carroll, a stockbroker who presented a puzzle to the neat-minded official.

> ‘First, I walked to the parade ground, where all the prisoners of war were. From there, we got into a bus and we were all driven to Stanley. When we got to Stanley, I presented my passport. The man looked at it and threw it on the ground. So I said, "What did you do that for?" He said, "You shouldn't be here, you're not an Englishman, you're an Irishman," So I said, "Well I'm a prisoner of war now." "No," he said, "you're not, you're not English." "No! I am not! I'm Irish." I picked up my passport and I said, "Thank you very much." He chuckled at my saying "Thank you very much," and he said, "Ireland is not in the war, Ireland is neutral." "But," I said, "I've been in Hong Kong for so many years and they treat me as a Britisher." So he said, "You mustn't stay here, you can go home."’

And this is how Carroll managed to pick up the threads of his civilian life, from pre-war stockbroker to wartime chicken farmer.

> ‘I went and bought a few laying hens and I started a chicken farm. I was staying in Caine Road, just below the Roman Catholic Cathedral. Every day, when I had eggs, I used to go to town to sell them. With that money I could buy rice, I could buy vegetables, fish or something like that.’

The Japanese officer helped Carroll by taking him to the Foreign Affairs Office in the Hongkong & Shanghai Bank, and later in getting rations of rice and meat. Even if this was an act of disinterested kindness, Carroll was denounced as a collaborator. It was the inevitable price of receiving the favours of Japanese officials.

> ❛ As I was driving down in the car, I saw a lot of Britishers on the road and they all shouted, "Collaborator!" So I just smiled at them; what could I say? I'm no more neutral than the man in the moon. ❜

Sometimes, that neutral moon would be obscured by clouds of suspicion. The Irish priest, or the welfare worker, anyone who came into contact with other Europeans, could so easily fall victim to Japanese fears of a spy network, secretly working against the occupying forces. Father Burke, one of a party of Jesuit fathers who kept the Wah Yan College open for students:

> ❛ People of all nationalities flocked to seek accommodation in the vacant classrooms as living quarters. Several were Chinese who had lost their homes during the battle. There were some Irish. We also had some Portuguese friends, some Italian and White Russian families. Then we were pleased to be able to offer refuge to four La Salle Brothers. The four of us Jesuits retired to a small portion of the building. We had a chapel and a small storeroom in which we kept some rice and tinned goods. We were just a skeleton crew, as it were, to grow more skeleton-like during the three and a half years of occupation. Most of the funds which we were able to get from the banks, in their last few hours of existence, had to be given to our staff as December salaries. This enabled some teachers and some domestic helpers to get away to China. But others couldn't leave, either because they had no friends anywhere outside Hong Kong, or because some of their children were too young for the perilous trek into China. They hoped that we could perhaps open the school and so be able to survive. One day, the Japanese officials posted on our doors a big notice, "Requisitioned by Authority". We didn't know what it meant. Were they going to take over the property? ❜

Unfortunately for the Jesuit priests, the Japanese inspected the College and seeing a number of trunks which were being stored there, threw one of them open. Out fell the College flag, tied to the flag of China and the Union Jack.

> ‘ When the captain saw the Union Jack, he stamped on it and called us enemies. We tried to explain but he was too excited. He persisted in calling us enemies. We were in a perilous situation. After some consideration, Father Joy and myself went off to the Supreme Court to try to get an interview with Colonel Noma. We complained that we were called enemies. We insisted that we were Third Nationals and that we had not infringed any of the regulations. The Colonel asked his aide many questions in Japanese and at length dismissed him. He then dismissed us. ’

Here, the matter rested. But arrests and rumours of arrests were in the air. Each day, in the spring of 1943, there was news of the arrest of Chinese and Europeans, and even of the Jesuit fathers.

> ‘ The news of the arrests of the Fathers and a Mr Monaghan spread amongst our friends in Hong Kong. The students were asking, why? We were alarmed when we heard that, in all, about 30 were arrested that same morning. Of these 8 or 9 were Europeans. The others were Portuguese and the majority were Chinese. Amongst those arrested were Mr Ginger Hyde and Mr Edmondson of the Hongkong & Shanghai Bank. We heard rumours that they were suspected of being in a spy ring. ’

Father Burke took food and visited the prisoners in the cells below the Supreme Court. The Fathers were spared, but Mr Monaghan, who had assisted the bankers, and 27 other unfortunates were executed in Stanley gaol. Father Burke tells of their fate and why they were executed:

> ‘ Mr Hyde and others thought it their patriotic duty to form a branch of the British intelligence service. They'd enrolled some Chinese and, without our knowing it, Mr Monaghan had joined. What their activities were I don't know, but later we found out that occasionally

some military escaped from the camps and there was some kind of organization which directed them to Shaukiwan where they were able to get boats and make their way to some island with guides to lead them to Free China. It seems that Mr Monaghan had something to do with these arrangements. Anyhow, the prisoners were examined and some of them got the water torture. Who would blame them if they confessed? After the war, Father Joy had an interview with an Indian policeman who said that he was present at the executions. He said that the 28 or so were made to form a circle in Stanley gaol. There was a block of wood in the centre with the executioner standing beside it. The first name called was Mr Hyde. He went to the block and one stroke of the sword beheaded him. Then the others were called, one by one, including poor Mr Monaghan. The fact that Mr Monaghan lived in our building must have deepened the suspicions of the Japanese against the rest of us. '

Before the discovery of the spy ring, the bankers had been kept down in Central and marched to the European banks each day to sign bank notes for issue and to help liquidate the deposits of their customers, so that the Japanese could drain the Colony of its wealth. They decided to keep secret records of every transaction.

' The compilation of these secret records, which became the main concern of the men for the eighteen months during which they were working with the Japanese, was not undertaken without misgivings. In the first place, it had to be done without attracting attention, not only from the Japanese but even from members of our own staff, and this was difficult in the cramped working conditions in the office. There was little doubt that, should the Japanese discover what was intended, the consequences would be unpleasant, if not serious, for those concerned. The first step in preparing these secret records was made easier by the Japanese themselves. They had been meticulous in stating their requirements only to the British officers, leaving it entirely to them to organize the clerical work involved. They had asked for several copies of the statements and it was a simple matter to instruct the clerks and typists to prepare two copies additional to those asked for. It was arranged that, if any questions were asked, the explanation would be given that the extra copies were being retained in case they were required subsequently. In this manner the compilation of a complete record of every transaction which passed through our books was maintained until June 1943, when the three British officers were transferred to the main civilian internment camp at Stanley. Even an adjusting account as at 31st December 1941 was taken out, although this was done as a mental exercise and to keep in practice as much as for record purposes. As time went by it became impossible to preserve complete secrecy and it must have been quite apparent to the Chinese staff what was being done. It is pleasant to record, however, that when put to the test, the loyalty of the Chinese was as steadfast as was that of the Portuguese. **9**

The bankers were also responsible for sending in parcels and, when the opportunity offered, money to the internees at Stanley. Some of this money was to buy drugs and vitamins, obtained by Dr Selwyn-Clarke and smuggled into the camps by his welfare organization. The locked vaults of the Hongkong & Shanghai Bank contained an even greater asset than money: six brown bottles of thiamine hydrochloride which Selwyn-Clarke was determined to obtain.

6 The main concourse of the Bank had been taken over by the Japanese military headquarters, but two courageous European members of the Bank staff, whom I've since tried unsuccessfully to trace, volunteered to get the vaults open and, with their help, the life-giving vitamin supply was carried out past the Japanese guard to my waiting ambulance. I was able to divide it between the Stanley internment camp, Bowen Road Military Hospital, the two main Chinese Hospitals and the POW camps at Shamshuipo, Argyle Street and North Point, in all of which the signs of beriberi were already apparent. On that occasion, the Japanese NCO, on guard with about five privates, cannot have known what was being spirited away; but I also wanted to get at the godown in Wanchai, where Hilda had stored the supplies that she had been forwarding, before the whole operation had to stop, to the embattled forces of free

China. From Stanley Camp I had received an urgent appeal to the welfare committee for a dental chair, certain surgical instruments and other medical supplies. Hilda and I knew that these were among her remaining stores but the godown had been sealed by the Japanese with a notice in Chinese characters to this effect: "Imperial Japanese army. Entry forbidden. Trespassers will be summarily shot."

To amateur smugglers, a dentist's chair was quite a challenge. For a fortnight I timed the movements of the Japanese patrol which covered the district and found them to be remarkably regular, so that I could identify a theoretically safe interval of thirteen minutes in which we would have to arrive at the godown, break into it, remove the required items to my ambulance, re-seal the entrance and quit the scene. I collected two volunteers from St Paul's French Hospital and at a given moment we tore away the notice board sealing the door. As quickly as possible, we got the heavy and bulky load of the chair into the ambulance, together with the other supplies. Then, just as we were ready to replace the board across the door, I saw the Japanese patrol marching straight towards us down the road. My heart sank like a stone. Apart from the prospect of being shot myself, I was responsible for the same danger facing my companions, for the ambulance, which would be lost to the welfare committee, and its contents, that were badly needed by the Stanley internees. The patrol was near enough for me to see that it was led by a Japanese naval officer, when, to my indescribable wonder and delight, it turned sharp left down a branch road. The marching steps grew faint and then silent. We finished our task and drove safely away. 〉

Although this humanitarian work was sometimes connived at by cooperative Japanese officers — and indeed one Japanese interpreter actually smuggled parcels and messages into camp for Selwyn-Clarke — it was fraught with danger. Sooner or later the Kempeitai would get wind of these transactions, with the inevitable consequence.

〈 It was the 2nd of May 1943 that brought the hammering on the door of St Paul's French Hospital soon after dawn. I was told that I was under arrest as head of British espionage in Hong Kong; that I had been sending messages to the British Army Aid group in Free China and to Mr John Reeves, the British Consul in Macau; and that these messages concerned the damage caused to Japanese ships by the US Pacific fleet, the movement of Japanese troops and other such matters. The Kempeitai unfortunately had means of obtaining the evidence that suited them from their victims and the charges that they decided to fasten upon me, which ran to about forty in all, involved others besides myself in extreme afflictions. I was to experience these methods too much in my own person ever to hold anything against those unfortunates who were compelled into false admissions that I had used them as agents for espionage. My admiration was all the greater for the courage of those who could not be suborned. **9**

Selwyn-Clarke, a brave and dedicated doctor, is reticent about his ordeal at the hands of the Kempeitai. But there is no denying the extreme cruelty of the tortures, which made men pray for the quick release of the executioner's sword. Selwyn-Clarke, of course, survived, and even insisted upon giving testimony on behalf of a Japanese officer at the post-war crimes trials. But the General Manager of the Hongkong & Shanghai Bank, Vandeleur Grayburn, was not so fortunate. He died, after being refused medical treatment by the Japanese, in Stanley gaol. However, the story of the bankers is not all black. They did pull off one spectacular success. They managed to smuggle out the entire financial records of the Hongkong Bank's last day of operations, before the Japanese take-over. One of the men involved in this was Charles Schafer:

6 They were typed on the thinnest onion-skin paper you could imagine, both sides, full margin, no space wasted anywhere, and the pile of records was about a half an inch thick . . .

Our first job, on working this out, was to go to the Japanese Civil Administrator with a long list of items that we were allowed to take when we were repatriated. We purposely put a lot of things on that list we knew they would object to. One of these was a trunk. The list read: trunks, binoculars, radios, cameras and other things of that nature and ended up with typewriters. We knew they wouldn't let us take any cameras. We weren't supposed to be taking any pictures at all, even if it was your own camera; and radios, you weren't supposed to listen to the radio. We knew they'd cross that off; and they didn't want any trunks. You were supposed to carry your baggage out. So it left just about typewriters. I guess, as an accommodation they said, "Yes." We then all went out and we bought typewriters. We bought identical typewriters, the old-fashioned portable kind that had black cases. You could take the top of the case off and release it at the back and, if you wanted to take the bottom off the case, you could press buttons and pull the typewriter right off the base. Well, Morton took all the typewriters and wrote our names in white paint. He lettered them across the top of the case, so we all had our names on our typewriters and we all had typewriters, which all looked like.

You know, we didn't want one of us to stand out because one had something that the others didn't have. Then Morton took his typewriter and tore the lining out of the bottom of the bottom part of the case, where they have these little projections that the typewriter would attach to. They stood up about 3/4 of an inch. We put the papers from the Hongkong & Shanghai Bank in between these posts. They fitted full to the edge. He then went to town and after a great deal of searching, found black silk, heavy black silk, that matched the black plastic leather case that they made in those days. Then, very carefully he cemented this silk over this whole thing with a little cardboard top to it, so that it looked like all the rest of the case bottoms. **'**

So, the Bank's records were hidden in John Morton's typewriter case; his colleagues, packed ready for repatriation, were also equipped, like good journalists, with their identical typewriters. When the time came to leave, Shafer and the others were asked to assemble at a pier on the Central waterfront.

' We got in the middle of the pier so that, whichever end of the pier they started to search everybody, we could see what kind of things they were looking for. Almost immediately, when the search by the Japanese gendarmerie began, the word was whispered to us, "They're looking in the lining of the clothes, you know. They're searching in the bottoms of the suitcases." As the tension increased, they got to us, and Johnny Morton, in his most professional magician-style proceeded to empty everything out of his suitcase and, in the course of doing this, covered up a number of things that he didn't want them to see, and, of course, the typewriters, which we kept by our sides. We then got on a bus and we were taken to Stanley. The *Asama Maru* was standing off the coast, a short distance away. At this point, the Japanese army were searching everybody, so it was a long wait in the hot sun while they finally figured out that we should line up alphabetically. That put Albert Fitch, at the head of our group. Well, Albert certainly hadn't thought that putting a carbon paper in with his typewriter would be bad at all — carbon paper was very hard to come by in those days. When they got to Fitch's typewriter, he opened it up and here was this carbon paper. The Japanese soldier doing the inspection held the carbon paper up to the light and could see, of course, that it had been typed on. There must be a code there somewhere. So there was a big wallahwallah; finally they said, you cannot take typewriters, and they confiscated our typewriters, all of them. 〉

The party boarded a tug and went out to the waiting ship, feeling at this point pretty low. Once aboard, they found the Japanese official who had originally decided that typewriters were to be included in the list of allowable possessions.

〈 We all rushed to him and said, "Mr Oda, you gave us permission to take typewriters and the Japanese army has taken our typewriters." Well, you could see his loss of face because here he was, the civilian administrator, and the army had countermanded his orders, as it were. He then said, "I will see about that." He stormed ashore and we kept watching. Just before we sailed, about 6 o'clock, the tug came alongside and we could see our typewriters, our names standing out like bill boards, being transferred aboard the ship. Albert Fitch was, I think, as young as I was, but he was impetuous.

He wanted to go right down and demand the typewriters, right then; but we restrained him. We said, "No, we'll wait, just as though nothing has happened." About five days out, the purser put a call in for us to appear at his office. He had decided that this was the time to hand us the typewriters. Well, we thanked him very much and rushed down to our room in the bowels of the ship, posted guards, rushed in an opened the typewriters. We could tell they had not been tampered with, so we had gotten out records through. **>**

These were the heroic gestures of resistance against the tyranny of Asiatic Imperialism. Of course, among the Chinese, these acts of defiance were multiplied a thousand times and more. Even the European housewife could, in her own way, make her token of resistance:

< Lane Crawford was open and the girls there in attendance were very, very nice, they were practically all Portuguese girls. The Japanese said that everybody must now speak Japanese or Chinese or not be served. So I used to go there and jabber in French. The girls didn't understand a word of what I said. As soon as the Japanese turned his back, I used to say, "A pound of sugar, please, quick." We had such a funny time. **>**

The Local Chinese Population
and the Occupation

(XVIII-XXII)

XVIII.

For the Chinese people living, or rather surviving in Hong Kong — the population in fact was reduced by famine conditions, enforced repatriation and a handful of escapes to about one-third from before the debacle — life had to go on as usual. It was true that the Japanese heralded their take-over of the British Colony as a Liberation from imperialist oppression; however, the Captured Territory and its people were to be exploited to aid the Japanese war effort in its desperate struggle against the superior power of the Allies. But if they could ever forget who were their new masters, Hong Kong citizens were to be reminded of the spiritual force of the samurai warriors by an overtowering War Memorial to the dead to be erected on Hong Kong Island. It was, however, doubly symbolic — that this grandiose monument was never completed.

(A. Birch)

XIX. These sketches, with their messages, might delude the latter-day viewer that 'The Great East Asian Co-Prosperity Sphere', of which Hong Kong was now part was not a dream.
However, the Hong Kong people's experiences of austerity, terror and coercion related in this book quickly dispel that illusion.
(*Tai Tung Wah Pao*, Vol. 2, no. 1, 1943. *Fung Ping Shan Library, University of Hong Kong Library*)

XIX. a. Of course. there was propaganda. The people were told there was 'a new prosperity'. the rich had fled leaving their clothing to the poor. 'the term unemployment is eliminated from Hong Kong'.
Rice. the staple of life. was no longer hoarded. There were fair rations for everyone.

XIX. b.
The people would be more dedicated, fitter through compulsory fitness sessions. Gone was the arrogant shouting of the British barbarians, it had given way to the rhythmic counting, one, two, three, of the exercises.

XIX. c.
Even the exigencies of the day were an opportunity for everyone to be self-reliant. Having no servants to perform the menial tasks, such as mending one's clothes, was a virtue to be encouraged. The hawkers on the street, eking out a living, were a convenience.

XX. The occupying authorities had their ways to secure collaboration. Prominent Chinese community leaders had the unenviable task, bequeathed to them by the defeated Hong Kong Government to try to protect the interests of the local people.

They had to walk a precarious tightrope between this duty and traitorous collaboration with the enemy.

No wonder this group of Hong Kong notables looked tense in the company of General Isogai, the first Japanese Governor of Hong Kong.

(A. Birch)

XXI. Japanese interior design in Government House, September 1945.　　(*Public Archives, Canada*)

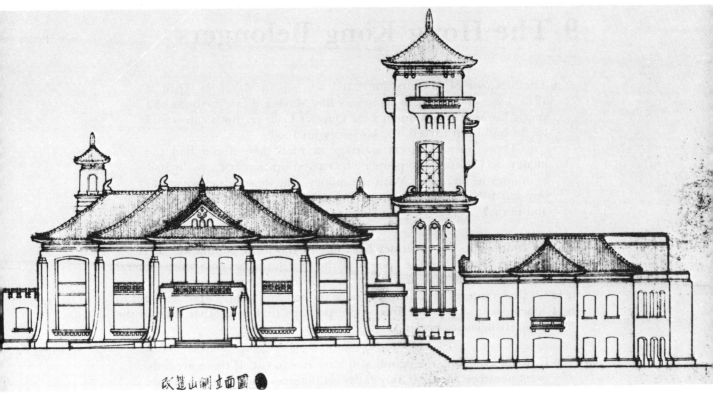

改建山側立面圖 ⚫

XXII. Government House, Hong Kong.
The lasting irony of the Occupation is the rebuilt Government House which replaced the undermined and collapsing structure of the nineteenth century. The young Japanese architect, Seichi Fujimura prepared the drawings for the present building which largely retained the original ground-plan.
The tatami, the Japanese baths and household shrines were removed soon after the end of the Occupation, but it still houses the Head of Government of Hong Kong, now a restored British territory.

(*Hong Kong, Information Services Department*)

9 The Hong Kong Belongers

‘The first case of cannibalism that I saw was in March or April of 1942. I was on my way to Causeway Bay Market. I saw the body of a young boy on the pavement near Queen's College. Both calves and thighs had been carved up, obviously for food.

There wasn't a great shortage of food then if you had the money, so I think those people who carved up that body really had no money to buy food. With the money that we still had we could buy star-fish, baby shark meat, vegetables and the occasional beef and pork.’

What a contrast to the promises held out to the local population of Hong Kong, as they listened to the speech of the new Japanese governor, General Rensuke Isogai, as he inaugurated the new order of Asian co-prosperity early in 1942. But whatever tantalizing dreams of food and plenty were held out to the Chinese, who appreciate food more perhaps than any other race in the world, the stringencies became tighter and tighter.

‘If rice is available, the people will have rice to eat. If there are only sweet potatoes, they will only eat sweet potatoes and if there are only beans, they will only eat beans.

This was Tanaka, the second Japanese governor, admitting the tightening grip of the American blockade of the China coast in 1944. By then Hong Kong's population had been reduced through official schemes of repatriation or, even more persuasive, the rumbling of empty stomachs, by more than one million souls. E.J. Carroll, the former stockbroker, recalls:

‘They starved a lot of them. In the last month of the war I used to come down Battery Path and walk straight along Queen's Road. Up against the pillars of all those buildings, you'd see a poor devil who you'd think was asleep, but he was dead.’

The first task of the occupiers was to purge Hong Kong of the excrescences of British Imperial rule which, they alleged, had so shamefully exploited and corrupted the Chinese people of Hong Kong. So, to purge and discipline the Chinese, who probably had never taken any of their rulers seriously to the point of total submission, the Japanese issued and fiercely enforced a whole mass of bureaucratic regulations to produce conformity. R.S. Ward was on the staff of the American Consulate in Hong Kong at that time. He somehow managed to record and analyse the propaganda and administrative measures which proliferated during this period. His book *Asia for the Asiatics* has more than a little irony in its title.

❛ On January 2nd 1942, the establishment was announced of the first regular governmental organization for the administration of the civil population of Hong Kong. It was called the Civil Department of the Japanese Army, later called the Civil Administration Department, to parallel the Military Administration Department. Major General Yisake, a ranking officer of the Occupying Army, was nominated its chief. Its office was established in the Hongkong & Shanghai Bank. It opened on January 1st. Some of the subordinate officers of the department were civilians and the clerical staff appears to have been largely Chinese. A Hong Kong bureau of the department — that is for Hong Kong Island — was subsequently opened under a civilian Japanese, one Mr Sumitani. In the department's first notice, issued on the day of its establishment, it declared that the Japanese army had seized Hong Kong with the object of sweeping out British and American influence from the Far East and establishing a new order in East Asia, freeing the races of the East. The Japanese army assumed responsibility, it asserted, for the protection of the lives and property of the Chinese people who should resume their businesses, fearlessly placing their confidence in the Japanese army.

A second notice, issued at the same time, stated that the Hong Kong government was now under the protection of the Japanese army and that, with the exception of British officials, all those formerly serving in the government ought to resume their functions as soon as possible. They should neither transgress the law nor act in a disorderly manner. If they were caught doing so, no leniency would be shown them. All labour and shops were instructed to resume business as soon as possible and not to act contrary to the law or else they would be dealt with.

A third notice informed the people of Hong Kong that, with a view to restoring conditions in the Colony, the Japanese army was doing its utmost to repair the water, electrical and gas systems but warned that any persons found wasting water would be dealt with according to Japanese army law without any leniency. **'**

Another Japanese officer, General Sakai, tried to soften the impact of occupation by trying to engage Chinese sympathy and support for the Asiatic crusade; but despite the soft talk, the harsh realities of the occupation were made clear.

' In his speech to the assembled Chinese General Sakai stated that: (1) The brave troops that he led had seized Kowloon and Hong Kong in a little over ten days, driving out the evil forces of the British. He had not been fighting the Chinese of Hong Kong for whom he had deepest sympathy and whom he hoped would understand the object of co-prosperity for all the races of great East Asia. He had not used artillery and large bombs in order to avoid hurting the common people and damaging the city. (2) The British Colonial administration planned only for its own profit, not caring about the life or death of the Chinese people. His audience should awaken to the fact that in this battle the British government used Chinese volunteers, Canadians and Indians in the front line, while the English soldiers were hiding in the hills. Investigation of the casualty list showed mostly coloured troops with very few Englishmen among them, from which it could be seen that English soldiers feared death and covet life. (3) The Chinese and Japanese are of the same people, have the same literature and belong to the same great East Asian race. The many Chinese in all the islands of South East Asia also were members of our race and he hoped that his words might also be transmitted to them, so that they too might join in the establishment of a greater East Asia. (4) He would spare no effort to make Hong

Kong and Kowloon a place where people may reside in peace. He asked his guests to form a local assistance committee to exert all their strength to help him.

The General then proceeded to a rough outline of his programme for the reconstruction of Hong Kong. The first item he listed was order. This was the responsibility of the military authorities but to avoid inconvenience to the populace, from the use of too many troops, the Chinese people were being re-employed and the people might organize their own self-protection guards under the direction of the officials.

The second important item which he indicated was to receive the attention of the military government was the currency. Describing it as the blood of business, he said that he had appointed people to deal with the matter, that there was reason for the non-acceptance of higher notes, that his guests, as the wealthy and influential element of the population, should, for the time being, tell all the people not to think of hurting other people or spread idle rumours.

On his third item — the relief of business — he expressed the hope that his guests would get together to help in settling the fuel and rice problems and that they would devise methods for this and apply to the administration for permission to carry them out.

Return to employment was the fourth problem the General discussed. Of it, he said, "Labour and business have stopped now, for many days. You should help in advising all classes of people to return to their employment at an early date."

The fifth and last item was "Cleaning up the City". Of this, the General told his guests that they should advise the people to start putting in order the places where they lived, thus helping the authorities to deal more easily with the problem of cleanliness. **'**

What this meant in practice is revealed by Miss Hui.

' Life became more and more difficult. Many left Hong Kong to go to Macau or the interior of China. Some of the very poor even starved. Dead bodies were often seen along the streets. A few months later, banks were opened. Each person was allowed to draw fifty Hong Kong dollars at the beginning, then 40% of the deposit from each account. The rate of exchange of Hong Kong dollars to Military Yen was 1 to 2 at the beginning and then 1 to 4. We lived a very simple and hard life for about two years, on rice, sweet potatoes with beans and vegetables and small fish which were normally used for feeding cats.

As always in a desperate war-time situation of shortages of food, clothing and fuel, there was a blackmarket. It had one merit — it helped keep people alive. A local citizen records his own experiences:

6 At that time I was the bread-winner for the whole family, although I was eight years old. I managed to make friends with the Japanese and climb in and out of the barracks very often. The Japanese soldiers were like any other soldiers, they needed money and many other things. So we did a little business with them — blackmarket business. There were lots of things in the barracks, lying about, that the Japanese wished to get rid of so I was the person to go up there to contact them and get them to sell. The goods were delivered to us in the middle of the night by Japanese soldiers and then were thrown over the wall and we had to go down to the street to pick them up. The next morning we'd take them to the market and sell them.9

Chan Sui Jin tells of having to burn precious possessions to cook food. He also remembers the increasing feeling of weakness, as starvation took its toll.

6I remember the very first effect of malnutrition was that we felt sleepy, all the time. We felt very sleepy and then we felt very itchy. I mean we scratched all over and yet it didn't stop. Then, after two or three months, we developed running sores which took a long long time to cure. In fact, they never cured until we left Hong Kong eighteen months afterwards. We were weak, we didn't even have the energy to raise a teacup. Of course there was no schooling, so there

122

was the sheer boredom of it, of staying at home feeling itchy, feeling weak and not knowing what to do. Eventually, the final and very unpleasant effect was that we developed severe cases of diarrhoea. Of course food was nowhere to be found and I remember we had only one solid meal of rice or congee a day. **'**

Chan tells of his family's removal from the scene of desolation and terror. It was a story to be repeated many many times.

'We were getting weaker and weaker, more running sores, more cases of malnutrition, more deaths in the street. Then my father summoned up his courage and we made our way to Sham Kong which was called Kwongchowwan then. We left Hong Kong by the *Silver Maru* in July 1942. **'**

Dr Li Shu Fan was more prominent in the public eye therefore more vulnerable to coercion to cooperate if he stayed. He ran, as well, a greater risk of punishment and reprisal if caught in an unsuccessful attempt to smuggle himself out of Hong Kong. He had to take more devious measures.

'I realized that the prelude to any successful plan of escape must be a psychological campaign to convince the Japanese that I had no intention of trying to get away. I must make them believe that I was in no spartan, patriotic frame of mind but was content to drift along. They must think that I was in fact beginning to crack under the strain and was about to slide into the loose, easy, pleasure-drugged existence for all leading Chinese who would collaborate. I set out therefore to persuade them that Dr Li Shu Fan was through with politics and patriotism and was going swiftly to the dogs. It was Friday night, July 30, and I remember thinking how wonderful freedom would be after eighteen months under the heel of the Japs. Towards morning I slipped on my fisherman's cap, an old brown jacket and blue trousers and looked in the miror to view my hard-earned suntan. Months previously I had decided that I would have to go disguised as either a fisherman or coolie, depending on whether I took the land or sea route. Then I had to acquire a deep tan or else my pale face would give me away. I started going about the streets without a hat, since even coolies wear hats against the tropical sun. Some people lifted their eyebrows at me but my trouble paid off. With a leathery face to match the old clothes, my disguise as a weather-beaten fisherman was complete.

At 5 a.m. Ah Chuk knocked quietly and came in. It was raining outside as I had hoped. I slipped on an old mackintosh and was ready. Until that moment Ah Chuk could not have known positively that I was escaping. When I told him, during my packing, that I was going to Shanghai, he insisted on accompanying me, whereupon I gave him money for his wife's support. Now the truth dawned upon him and though the escape route into interior China was literally paved with the lives of refugees, he staunchly did not hesitate to come along. When we got out to the car, my chauffeur also guessed the game. I slipped him my last bundle of useless Military Yen notes and told him to drop Ah Chuk and myself off at my town clinic, where we had to pick something up before proceeding to the steamer for Canton. I dismissed him on arrival as I did not want him to know my movements, in case the Japs questioned him. Ah Chuk then hailed two passing rickshaws and we proceeded to a certain wharf, which I previously noticed was guarded by only one gendarme. A long queue of coolies, both men and women, were lined up in the drenching rain on the wharf. Because of the terrible weather, the gendarme did not arrive in time to see this first ferry shove off. We got aboard safely and crossed without incidents. In the downpour we made our way through the Kowloon streets to the house of Hong Cheong's mother, where my luggage had been kept. How good it felt to get into dry clothes, rest and have a hot and hearty meal. But we could not stay long. In the company of a young smuggler, whom Hong Cheong had hired to guide us, we left the house and started across the hills to the peninsula coast. We made the dangerous trip so easily that I began to think that our escape was assured. At the promontory I walked out alone to the rocky point, as Hong Cheong and I had arranged. He was to be somewhere near the point in a one-mast sampan, with an old fisherman smuggler and his family. There was however, no sampan and no Hong Cheong. Several shore patrols were walking along the beach. While I nervously waited, not knowing what to do, a fisherman came trudging up. As he passed me, he mumbled, "Are you a fisherman?" Anxious and irritated, I snapped, "Mind your own business." He stopped, scratched his grey hair, looked at me and then said, "It's good weather, shall we go fishing?" The words were sweet music in my ears. They were the passwords which Hong Cheong and I had arranged. I signalled Ah Chuk and we followed the old fellow down the beach to a sampan where Hong Cheong was waiting. We put off from the shore hurriedly to get away from the beach patrols and headed through the channel for the coast of free China.

This was the dilemma facing prominent Chinese families and even not so prominent members of the Chinese community: if they stayed, to protect their own interests, or to protect those of the community generally, they realized that they would appear to be traitors. Some of the leading figures had been astutely appointed by the Japanese to head local representative committees and district bureau to give the appearance of local representation. In fact it was to ensure local responsibility for any misdeeds of resistance against the occupiers. Ironically, some of these men who appeared to be collaborators, had been asked by officials of the defeated Hong Kong government to take up this impossible role. For them it was like walking a tight-rope. Small wonder that they refuse to talk about their experiences today. They simply say there's nothing of interest to anybody else. But some could, after qualms of loyalty, take up minor positions under the Japanese. Another medical man, Dr Zia:

While classes for Japanese lessons were still going on, there was a circular issued by the medical department inviting applications from doctors to take up medical posts in Hainan Island. I went to the bureau the next day and interviewed the Director who introduced me to the chief interpreter and the head of the department, a Japanese returned student. They let us fix up my monthly family allotment, rice allowances, gave all information about the nature of the work and told me to get in contact with the office as often as I could. I returned home and told my wife that I had accepted the job. My wife took the news half-heartedly, with an expression of consolation combined with perplexity. She was consoled because the family got protection but she was worried because my future was in absolute darkness. After pausing for a while she spoke impressively, "Can't you withdraw your application? How am I going to look after the home and the children and pass the lonely years?" I replied, "This is a time of emergency and as long as you have got enough money for the family we should all be content. The Japanese have great respect for doctors and, when you work for them, they treat you as one of their own men. The Jap soldiers fought because they were under orders from the Generals not because they had personal hatred against all Chinese. If you have fair feelings for them they do not kill you without reason, like savages do. In this wide world it is the language bar and politics which make people of different nations treat each other like aliens. I can withstand a hard life and loneliness will vanish when you understand that there is a group of doctors and nurses going together," I explained, and convinced her. **'**

Not until we can break down the natural reticence of the survivors of this terrible period of strain and sacrifice, shall we fully know the extent of the proud secrets of resistance of the local men and women of occupied Hong Kong. Acts of heroism were probably not uncommon. Dr Lee recalls:

' Looking back I recall an amusing incident, though I now realize I was very lucky then to have got away with it. It involved a short-wave radio which a friend of mine gave me in the University hostel. At that time, the Japanese military authorities issued a proclamation saying that it was illegal to use short-wave radios. I carried this radio in my hands all the way from the University down Bonham Road and Caine Road, to Central district and then made my way towards my destination which was Tin Hau Temple Road in Causeway Bay. I knew that there was a fixed sentry point at the foot of Tin Hau Temple Road, so I thought I would avoid this sentry by going down a side lane up in the hill of Tai Hang. When I got to the position where I thought I would be able to by-pass this sentry I was shocked to find that he had changed his sentry point from the foot of Tin Hau Temple Road, to further up, where I had no choice but to go through because he had seen me already. I hesitated for a few seconds as to whether I should pass him and then decided that if I were to turn back he would suspect something. I decided that I would put on a bold front and pass by him and, as I did so, I turned towards him and made a deep bow and he signalled me on to pass. I realized that I was very lucky that he was either in a lazy mood or had no interest in being careful about people passing the sentry point. Looking back now, I realize I was so fortunate to have escaped what might have been a certain death penalty. **'**

The people of Hong Kong gave succour to the starving prisoners of war in the forced labour gangs working in the city outside the camps. They brought parcels to the soldiers in Shamshuipo and to the civilians in Stanley. The least risk they ran was that they would be beaten up. As one volunteer remarked, just thinking about those acts of loyalty and love helped to save his and his comrades' lives.

10 Links with the Outside World

Even if the impregnable fortress was now a prison, the doors to the goal could never be bolted completely. There were escapes over the wire. People mysteriously melted away, despite the guards, to Macau and Kwongchowwan. All these brave endeavours required careful planning and contact with the outside world in order to be successful. For those like Gimson, whose duty it was to remain in the occupied Colony — to keep the British flag flying (and that symbol of loyalty and resistance was secretly buried away from irreverent hands) — it was vital to have a radio link with Chungking. This would be used to take steps for the unquestionable liberation of Hong Kong.

The following description of the necessarily elaborate organization which was necessary to maintain the link is described in a report written immediately after liberation by Lieutenant W.H.P. Chatley:

Secret and confidential report on wireless activities and escape plans in the civilian internment Camp Stanley, afterwards known as the Military Internment Camp.

The original plans to establish and maintain a wireless set in Stanley civilian internment camp were made by Mr. J. Fraser, Defence Secretary of the Hong Kong Government, and certain members of the Cable and Wireless Company, immediately after the capitulation of Hong Kong on 25th December 1941, and during the interim period, before the Japanese authorities interned all the British subjects inside the camp. As a consequence, arrangements were made for all of the component parts of the wireless sets to be brought into the internment camp, hidden in the baggage of various civilians, mostly employees of Cable and Wireless, who were moved into the camp by the Japanese authorities in late January and early February 1942. These plans were hidden for at least two months, until the Japanese procedures of roll call and searches were familiarized. The first set was assembled, tested and maintained by Messrs Reece and Waterton of Cable and Wireless, who installed it in the chimney of the kitchen of their flat on the top floor of Block

15, Indian quarters. Heavy, black velvet curtains were hung over all windows and doors of the flat, ostensibly for blackout precautions. This flat was a third-storey flat with access to the roof and was approached by only one stairway and only one entrance door, which could be locked. Nightly watches were arranged to listen in to the Chungking and New Delhi broadcasts principally. The main items from these broadcasts were scribbled down in abbreviated longhand, in complete darkness, by the person listening, who of course used head-phones and not a loud-speaker. Mr J. Fraser, Defence Secretary, Hong Kong, then organized the procedure whereby every morning he would transcribe these hastily written notes into longhand on his typewriter, one copy only. at an appointed rendezvous. Mr Fraser detailed me to act as his staff officer in this respect. I prepared situation maps of the western, middle-east, and eastern fronts, which were kept as up-to-date as possible. These maps I retained in my possession and I was entirely responsible for their upkeep and safekeeping. I checked and traced name places from the limited number of atlases in the camp. I also had to arrange the rendezvous mentioned above and carried verbal messages to the various members of the wireless inner circle. By this procedure, the key people avoided being seen talking together, a precaution which served us in good stead for many months in a camp where, if two or three people had talked together for any length of time, it was bound to be commented on. **'**

Then, of course, to know the situation in order to erase the lies of Japanese propaganda about their great victories in the Pacific, men risked their lives listening surreptitiously to the B.B.C.. The internees' morale was undoubtedly greatly boosted when they heard the news over the secret radio of the surrender of the leader of the Fascist axis-alliance, Nazi Germany, on 8 May 1944.

' This is London. The Prime Minister, the Right Honourable Winston Churchill:

"Yesterday morning at 2.41 a.m. at General Eisenhower's headquarters, General Jodl, the representative of the German High Command and of Grand Admiral Dönitz, the designated head of the German State, signed the act of unconditional surrender of all German land, sea and air forces in Europe to the Allied Expeditionary Force."**❜**

Michael Wright, an officer with the Gunners, spent his enforced idleness in the Argyle Street Camp learning Chinese characters and shorthand. This was a very useful combination for intelligence work in captivity, as he explains:

❛The sergeant in my battery was a shorthand teacher in civilian life and at that time we all thought that the Japanese would be defeated in Malaya and it was only a matter of a few months before Hong Kong would be relieved. One was looking for something short and sweet to keep oneself occupied. Three of us decided that we would learn shorthand from Charlie Dragon who had a wonderful name and was a very good instructor. We were only able to spend four or five hours a day practising, and I got up to 50 w.p.m. I never got beyond that. This, in fact, led to my being fairly useful because one of the Japanese sentries was smuggling in a Chinese newspaper. I might say here that we got no news at all, except rumours, and it was of great value to get this Chinese newspaper smuggled in. The newspaper was translated by a brilliant Chinese scholar, Ken Barnett, who used to write the translation out in longhand. Of course, every time he finished writing out a sentence he had to find his place again in the newspaper. It all had to be done surreptitiously under his bedclothes or in a dark corner. One day, he asked me what my shorthand speed was and I said about 50 w.p.m. He said, "Well, that's about the speed I can translate the paper," and so for the next several months he and I and another chap would be closeted with Barnett for half an hour or forty-five minutes and he would read out the news. We would take it down in shorthand and then go round the huts to read it out.**❜**

Private Gomez of the Volunteers knew about this grapevine.

❛We had a radio in camp so a lot of the information of the outside world came to us. The Japanese suspected that there was a radio so that we had umpteen searches. Each time, the set was carefully dismantled, with each person carrying one-part and then afterwards it was reassembled again so that fortunately it was never found. If it had been found, I'm sure some people would have died. Another source of news was working parties. Every time we came back from a working party, somebody would give us some news. News was always cheerful — sometimes I suspected it was the camp's psychologist at work. **'**

As Canon Martin in Stanley said:

' When the Colony was overwhelmed on the Christmas Day of 1941 both press and radio of course came to a sudden and dramatic stop. It was only when they were no longer available that we came to realize what an important place they occupied in our lives and how much we depended upon them. I speak for the camp at Stanley, for I was part of its administration and I can testify that our hunger for dependable news became second only to our hunger for food. It was the absence of reliable news which encouraged the spread of every sort of rumour, some of which were quite fantastic, but people lapped them up nevertheless. It soon became clear that the only possible way of obtaining the sort of news for which we longed and languished was to get a radio receiving set going somehow. Although everybody knew that this was a highly dangerous business and that the consequences of discovery would almost certainly be fatal, there were those who were prepared to take the risk. Prison camps are known as places where human ingenuity had to discover how to do the impossible and so, in due time, there was a radio receiving set working in Stanley Camp, many parts of which had been smuggled in from Hong Kong. As a matter of fact, there were at least three radio sets working, but only one became really known. Although people were sworn to the strictest secrecy, and urged to be absolutely discreet, the news began to get around and what a difference it made to people when they could feel that what they were getting now was not rumour but the real thing. Such news was a mighty booster of camp morale but disaster and stark tragedy overtook us.

It is sad to have to say that those camps had their traitors as well as their men of courage and genius and Stanley, with its people of so many nationalities, was no exception. Of course our captors gave every encouragement to informers. So the betrayer — perhaps I ought to say betrayers, I'm sure there was more than one — the betrayers, passed on to the enemy the details of our radio set. The Japanese bided their time, until they felt that they had obtained all the information they required, then they pounced, and made a number of arrests, two of the most prominent being Mr W.R. Scott, who was the head of the intelligence department of the Hong Kong Police, and Mr J.A. Fraser, who had been the Defence Secretary. During the night following the arrests, the radio was buried on the hillside, in a desperate attempt to destroy the evidence, but the Japanese knew exactly where it was buried and by whom. The betrayers had been at work again. The unfortunate culprit was marched to the spot and made to dig and dig until the set was unearthed. The camp of course was stunned by this turn of events and, as the weeks went by, every effort was made to discover what was happening or what was likely to happen to the prisoners. We got to know nothing. However, on the afternoon of the 29th October 1943, my wife happened to be crossing the prison area when the gates opened and a van drove out. As the van passed her, some English voices called out, "Goodbye. Remember us to everybody." The van drove on to a nearby hill overlooking the beach, and in full view of a certain section of the camp the radio victims were executed and buried. They were not decapitated, they were shot, and this, said the Japanese, was a special privilege to them. After the surrender of the Japanese, I visited the cells where my friends had awaited their fate and from which they went out to give their lives and it was with very deep emotion indeed that I read the messages they had written on those cell walls. There I paid my tribute to a group of brave men who had paid so heavy a price in their endeavour to bring something of hope into the drab lives of their fellow prisoners through the medium of radio. **'**

News was hope, and hope was life. Though the attempt to smuggle news into the camps was fraught with the gravest risks, information about the outside world was a weapon of war more potent than any firearm. Bombardier Weller explains:

> As time went on, and of course we had no radios in Japan, not like Hong Kong, the only way we could get any news was to steal newspapers from the factory, which our people who could read Cantonese were able to translate. These newspapers gave us a pretty good idea of what was going on. It was always quite exciting because the word would go round the factory that something big had happened. Then you had to get one and this was always rather a risky job. We always managed to get one somehow. Rather funnily, at the end of the war they found the maps that we had drawn and how we had known exactly how things were going, in Germany and the Pacific. When we told them we were merely reading their newspapers, they were very annoyed. But anyway, as I say, we did find out and then, of course, as the Americans moved closer to the Marianas and Saipan, we knew that we were going to start getting the bombs and sure enough our first B29s appeared over Nagoya. From there on we were bombed fairly severely.

Captain Bothelo, speaking Cantonese, had an advantage which was too valuable not to exploit.

> One party went out from Shamshuipo at that time to Kai Tak. I went up to this party. Normally, officers who could speak a bit of Chinese went out with these parties to try and get some information. On this occasion, we went out with the party and came back with the news — who got it I can't say because we never mentioned names on those occasions. There were some black sheep in camp. We came back with the news that the Japanese had suffered a very severe naval disaster. I think it was a battle, of the Coral Sea. We heard this and it was confirmed because the Japanese used to send us Japanese papers for the purpose of propaganda and we could read between the lines. I think that was the occasion when the very famous Japanese Admiral, who was compared at that time to Nelson, was shot down in a plane.

The one constant, unbroken, ever-reliable life-line with Hong Kong however, was the British Army Aid Group. Colonel Ride had been determined
to create this vital link with Hong Kong. aiding escapes. bringing medicine and
relief secretly into the Japanese-held territory and, at the same time, securing
valuable intelligence information for the US Air Force bombers which were
visibly bringing defeat nearer, everyday, to the Japanese army of occupation in
China and Hong Kong.

Paul Tsui, who was to win the M.B.E. for his services in the B.A.A.G.,
tells about the contribution of that unique organization:

> ❛The actual British Army Aid Group came into existence, I would
> say, by the 1st of July [1942]. I was sent down to Wai Chow to
> establish a 'F.I.G.', that is, Field Intelligence Group. I took a team
> of ten down with me, of whom four were to be runners between Ku
> Kong and Waichow to dispatch the messages. I was to be stationed
> at Waichow, and the remaining six were sent to the occupied
> territories at home. Two would be runners between Hong Kong and
> Waichow and four would be operating in Hong Kong. That was the
> first official team of the British Army Aid Group's Field Intelligence
> Group.❜

The network, for planning and assisting escapes from the camps, depended
upon contacts with the world outside the barbed wire. The British Army Aid
Group cooperated with Chinese guerrillas operating in the New Territories
and in Southern Kwangtung to run its milk-run in and out of Hong Kong.

A local Portuguese Volunteer prisoner of war heard about the dire
consequences of failure of plans to escape from Shamshuipo.

> ❛The only other incident of escape that I knew of, at the time, was
> told to me by my friend, Bob Sheehan. He was an Irishman who had
> been in the British army and who was middle-weight champion of
> the British army at boxing. He was a very brave man and he told me
> that he had been in touch with Captain Ford of the Royal Scots,
> Lieutenant Gray, and an Indian army officer called Ansari. These
> three officers were plotting with Chinese guerrillas, through truck
> drivers who were delivering rations in camp, to blow up the

perimeter fence on the northern side of the camp. The Chinese guerrillas would make a foray into our camp and try to take away as many prisoners with them as they could. I think this one misfired because not long afterwards Captain Ford, Lieutenant Gray and Captain Ansari were taken away from our camp and were taken to Stanley. We heard, after after the war, that they had been tried and executed by the Japanese. We heard also that the execution was not done in the usual way of beheading. The Japanese respected these three officers so much that they granted them the very special privilege of being shot by a firing squad. **'**

Not all their work was in Hong Kong: Paul Tsui described the organization of which the B.A.A.G. was part.

' B.A.A.G. was a military organization working in South China from early '42 to the end of '45. It had a definite war establishment and was controlled by the D.M.I. that's the Director of Military Intelligence, G.H.Q., through the Military Attaché, British Embassy, Chungking until early 1945. Thereafter it became an integral part of the British troops in China under the G.O.C., British Troops, China. For a period of over 12 months, during 1942 to 1943, we quartered, fed and trained over 300 Chinese ex-members of the Hong Kong Volunteer Defence Corps, the R.N.V.R, the Hong Kong Chinese Regiment, and the R.A. and R.E. We also had civilian escapees from Hong Kong. These troops were kept at Headquarters in Kweilin, until instructions were received from the Admiralty and War office for their disposal. **'**

As the end of the war drew nearer, it became more imperative to use the link with Macau to receive instructions from London on exactly how to establish the authority of the British Government again in Hong Kong. This was both an urgent and difficult task. The local population was ready to wreak vengeance upon the Japanese troops and officials. The prisoners of war in Stanley and Shamshuipo were in no condition to enforce law and order. They themselves probably had a bit of private reckoning to attend to anyway. The Chinese connection, tenuous as it had been, now seemed an ominous threat to the resumption of British rule. In fact, there were large bodies of Chinese troops, under the command of local warlords, encamped in the vicinity of Kowloon, ready to march in if the right price were paid to return Hong Kong to China. The future of Hong Kong would depend upon the precarious mission of one man, Arthur May, a Public Works Engineer, to proceed to Macau and bring back instructions, via the British Consul there, on how to take swift action and reinstate the Crown Colony. Arthur May is too modest a man to be willing to recount his part in this, a crucial episode in Hong Kong's history. But again that doctor with an iron will, 'Septic' Selwyn-Clarke, as his enemies named him, can tell us something of what happened on that mid-August morning in 1945.

‘There was no means of direct communication with London; but I could still count on the resourcefulness of Arthur May, for whom I borrowed 2,000 Yen with the idea that he should make his way to Macau by sea and ask Mr Reeves, the British Consul, to get in touch by submarine cable with the British Ambassador in Lisbon, who could in turn signal London for the Colonial Secretary's instructions. Arthur went off to the Kowloon waterfront and hired a sampan for the journey which, as he afterwards reported to me, was not without incident. Off Tai O they were stopped by pirates and, to avoid involving his crew, he talked the pirates into an agreement to take him to Macau, on the promise of a reward, allowing his own sampan and crew to return to Hong Kong. Presently his new conveyors came up with a larger pirate vessel and anchored beside it to eat their midday meal and gossip with the crew, having first persuaded Arthur to hide under the floor-boards. After what seemed an interminable time, during which Arthur, cramped in the bottom of a bobbing boat and with evil-smelling bilge water lapping over him, was violently sea-sick, they cast off again, released him from his misery and eventually landed him at Macau where they got their reward. Arthur presented himself at the British Consulate. The line of communication was opened, and on the 23rd of August, with no liberating force as yet in sight, there was a satisfactory reply for Mr Gimson, who at once applied himself with exemplary energy to the task of getting the wheels of government turning again.’

There is far more to be told about the liberation of Hong Kong, especially during that crucial fortnight until Admiral Harcourt and his fleet sailed into Hong Kong harbour, blowing the last of the Japanese suicide squads out of the water. One thing can be said with certainty now. If Hong Kong had been completely isolated or absorbed into the Empire of the Rising Sun, if there had been none of these perilous and fragile contacts with the outside world, with China and through to London, the very heart of British resistance, it is more than probable that we would not be telling this story of Hong Kong's survival today.

11 The Japanese Exile

There are only a few survivors from the slave ship, the *Lisbon Maru*, alive in Hong Kong today. There are only one or two more of those who were transported to the prison camps in Japan, who survived that ordeal and who are alive here today to tell their tale. The story of the Hong Kong prisoners of war who were taken to bondage in the homeland of the Samurai warrior has never been told.

What were the feelings of those chosen for the slave passage? Fear, certainly, especially after the sinking of the *Lisbon Maru* and of many other such ships by the American Navy, which was unable in this situation to discriminate between friend and foe. The blockade of the China coast was vital for the final defeat of the enemy, Japan. Fear, too, of the Japanese population, unused to having foreigners in their midst. The prisoners might well be afraid of the understandable feelings of hatred and revenge from the population, itself now suffering the atrocities of war with the massive firebomb raids and the horrors of Hiroshima and Nagasaki. In fact, the Japanese civilian population — which was submissive but had its own code of correct behaviour — showed compassion to the prisoners. There were many paradoxes. Jack Edwards, today a champion for the rights of those prisoners, although not taken prisoner in Hong Kong was with them in the camps. He describes the paradoxes and the conditions which gave rise to them.

‘I read a remarkable story only last year of a man whom I met in London, who similarly was sunk on one of those ships. He related to me a story of how he picked up a Japanese women with a baby in the water. He and his mates reckoned that if they managed to get this Japanese women and baby with them on a piece of wood, when the Japs came along, they'd stand a chance of being picked up by a Jap destroyer. But the woman slipped off the wood and they were left with the baby. Eventually, the Jap destroyer came along, picked up the baby and left them in the water. To this day, he's haunted. This is true; he's haunted by the thought of whether that baby survived. I've said to him, "Why don't you write to a Japanese newspaper, they'd probably give you the Order of the Golden Sword, if the baby is still alive." This is the sort thing that happened, you know. There is something that people don't quite understand in the British character. **'**

This next episode took place in Burma, where thousands died in the building of the notorious bridge on the River Kwai and on the railway itself. It could have taken place anywhere and shows how the feelings of national hatred can be washed away by a feeling of common humanity only experienced by those sharing the sufferings of war.

' On the Burma-Siam railway, a trainload of Japanese wounded came along one day from the Burma front and pulled up alongside a Japanese POW camp where all these prisoners were. The stench was appalling, because the wounded were lying in open trucks, their wounds untended, crying for water. Do you know what these British POWs did? They gave them water. Now that's typical of the characters of the men who were in those camps. I must confess I only found one Japanese ever, in the whole of my three and half years' captivity, who showed compassion, only one. We were sleeping head to toe in our huts. We had to sleep head to toe because we felt this was a way of trying to keep down disease. We wouldn't be breathing towards each other at night time. The Japanese guards used to walk along where our heads were, on a catwalk in this bamboo hut. This particular night, I was suddenly woken by somebody tapping my forehead and I looked up. There was a Jap standing over me with a rifle and bayonet. I thought "trouble" because I was the hut leader. He opened my mouth with his finger and pushed in a small rice biscuit. I think that that Jap was moved with compassion because it was about a fortnight after I'd been very badly interrogated. I think that probably he felt sorry for what had happened. I think he remembered, you know, and maybe in the hours of that early morning he passed me and saw me lying there, and suddenly he felt he had to do something. But that's one of the silly things you remember amongst all the bad things that happened. We were peculiar societies, extraordinary societies. We fluctuated between a few hundred and twenty thousand but we stuck unswervingly to the British way of life and its principles. You know, we used to go to work and come back and nurse the sick, try and force rice down our comrades' throats — those who were dying — to keep them alive. Everybody looked ugly with disease and beriberi but we put up with each other, we had to. Everybody shared the food. Every man could do what he liked. The golden rule was: you could do what you liked so long as you did nothing to bring harm to your pals. **'**

Nobody seems to know exactly how many camps there were in Japan for the Allied soldiers, sailors and airmen taken prisoner. There were camps, too, in Taiwan and Korea where Sir Mark Young, the captured Governor of Hong Kong, gallantly resisted blandishment and torture which followed the signing of the surrender document, which had firmly sealed the years of captivity for the Colony. Jack Edwards speaks of communities of up to twenty thousand men. W.J. Howard was in a number of camps with around four hundred men. He thought there were prison camps in each Japanese city, and he could be right, for the prisoners were drafted to work in munitions factories, the docks, shipyards and coalmines. But the prisoners might be in ignorance of each other's existence. Howard, for instance, did not discover there was another camp for American POWs just down the road until the end of the war. Bob Yates, a gunner from the Mount Davis Battery, describes working conditions in these city camps:

' We heard that the Allies had told the Japanese they knew they were holding prisoners of war in the main cities and employing them on war work. In one case, they even built a prisoner of war camp between two dry docks, presumably so that, if the Allies bombed the shipyard, they would kill the prisoners as well. By that time the people, the higher-ups in Japan, knew that they were going to lose the war. This was March 1945 and Tokyo and Yokohama were being very heavily bombed at that time. They decided to move us all to various places in Japan. I remember the night we got to Tokyo railway station. There was nothing else but prisoners of war there — I don't remember how many thousands there were — but they piled us into a train and other people into various other trains, and away we went up north to a place called Kamaishi, which was a large steel works. We didn't know where we were going to, of course, and no matter how bad conditions were, as prisoners, you always tend to dread moving, because you think, well, things can't be much worse. But then again, inwardly, you think, well, maybe they can. So we had no idea what conditions were going to be like in this camp. It turned out that they were actually worse, mainly because in the camps we'd been in most of us were regular soldiers, I don't know what it was, but we seemed to stick together, if one chap was a bit down, well, the others would pull him up and this applied to everyone of us. But when we went to this other camp, there were Dutchmen in there from the Dutch East Indies and they appeared to be pretty well cowed by the Japanese. A lot of it rubbed off on us. However, I can honestly say that I don't recall any of our chaps being really cowed. Of course, when conditions are strict like that, when you first move in, it's a gradual process to get them to ease off. **'**

But, in the matter of food, things did not get any better. Bob Yates again:

' Conditions were even worse as regards food, because, by that time, Japan was getting very short of food. We were eating boiled chrysanthemums or at least chrysanthemum soup. I believe at that time in Tokyo the vegetable ration was one cabbage leaf per person every four days. That was for civilians so we couldn't have expected anything better. **'**

Bob Yates served as a regular soldier in Hong Kong from 1938 and had been taken prisoner, returned to his former barracks at Shamshuipo and then shipped to Yokohama in 1942. The camp he was put into was not intended for prisoners.

' It was a baseball stadium in Yokohama and we were under the stands. Every morning we used to go out onto the grass part of the stadium for roll-call. We were assigned to various working parties: for instance, one was in a peanut oil factory, another was unloading ships in the harbour, mainly coal ships and iron ore.

I think we worked from 7 in the morning. We used to parade until 6 at night and, I'm not sure now whether it was half an hour or an hour, I'll give them the benefit of the doubt and say an hour lunch-break.

We were definitely undernourished. I kept a diary of all the meals we ever had in prison camp and unfortunately it was destroyed in the bombing in the last camp I was at. In Japan, rice was very short and in the main, we got boiled barley and something called Kaoliang. It was a red millet. We used to call it birdseed. On very rare occasions we did get fish and we got a local Japanese turnip which was called Dica.'

Here, in this land of the oriental enemy, German technicians in the shipyards, who of course were also enemies of the British, shared a common western remembrance of Christmas.

'When I first went there, we went to work in a repair yard. They also built ships there, but it was mainly a repair yard — Asano Dock Yard. When we went in there, there was a German ship. Of course, we weren't supposed to go near it. The German crew used to call some of us on to the ship however. They used to give us a meal and they were very sympathetic towards us. You know we appreciated what the Germans did for us. The first Christmas we were there they even sent in a Christmas tree with lights and a sum of money for us.'

Jack Weller also describes his experience in the camp and in the factory.

'People worked in different factories: some in machine ships, some of those who had skills were on lathes, others like myself were only fit to fetch and carry. Others, less fortunate gentlemen, were in the moulding shop which was probably one of the dirtiest jobs imaginable. That was really a very dirty job. We stayed in Nagoya until May of '43, and then, for some unknown reason, they divided the camp and didn't tell us where we were going. In fact, it was the

142

day after VE day. We knew that there was victory in Europe, there was a big cheer that night. Our camp commandant had come in and said "Gentlemen, the war is over in Europe." The next day, we were off, and we turned up in a place on the west coast of Japan, a place called Toyama, very beautiful. It was still mighty cold. We were there in May and the mountains were still covered in snow. We hung around there for about a week because they didn't seem to know what to do with us. Up until then the place hadn't had an air-raid at all. Eventually they took us to the factory and we started work, same old thing. We were building tractors this time or helping to. **'**

The prisoners of course were not always helpless. They were forced to work to further the Japanese war effort but they could also sabotage production. Mr Roy Lance, a volunteer, talks about how they tried to bring the trains to a halt.

' We were sent off to work in a locomotive factory, where I worked in the moulding section. We had the job of moulding the big wheel, the driving wheel of a locomotive. Other people were given different jobs but among us was a very good saboteur, an Australian engineer who you would never ever think was a saboteur, he was so innocent looking. He caused more damage than anybody else to those finished locomotives. Of course other people would do things too, like leaving bits of rock or cloth in the boiler tubes and then the trains blew up in Manchuria. They used to come back looking as if they had been hit by a mine. This was all due to the sabotage going on in the factory. When we got to the factory the Japanese there were cockahoop. The war was going to last for a hundred years and they were all very cheerful. They were given a work norm which they exceeded because they'd been promised more money and more rations. When the money and rations didn't come they eventually slackened off, leaving the POWs working in the factory. Well, they had to work, because if they didn't work the guards would come around and knock 'em silly. A few months after we arrived there the air-raids started. The planes used to come in from the sea. Strangely enough they would pivot right over our heads and make a bee-line for Nagoya or Osaka as the case may be. It was very funny. In the beginning, if we were in the factory and an air-raid was coming, we would be hustled off and sent back to camp. Eventually, the air-raids were so bad we used to stay in camp for four or five days at a stretch. Our factory was rather badly damaged in one of the air-raids, so we never went back to work there again. Some of us were shipped off to other camps and some of us went to a smaller factory of the same locomotive factory where we did maintenance work on engines. But soon after that interest lagged. The Japs weren't interested in working and, of course, we weren't very interested either. **'**

There was one question on the minds of prisoners, wherever they were. In Japan this question was posed in the form of a prayer:

How long, O Lord, how long? How long O Lord, how long?
No answers given.
Again this plaint assails the gates of heaven.
How long, O Lord, can men endure the fate of blasted hopes,
    defeat the vengeful hate?
How long can spirit live and will survive and keep the flickering
    flame of faith alive?
In thralldom dark, depressed with cankering care,
How long can hope contend with black despair?
How long, O Lord, how long for doom to shame,
We're waiting still for help that never came,
Escaping death, alive to wonder why,
In living death, a thousand times to die.
Proud valour mute when base derision mocks,
Rank degraded where yoke make to the ox,
Life's crowning goal of honoured high command
Now a coolie slave, a chunkle in my hand.

How long, O Lord, how long?
For all I know my loved ones may be dead, long months ago.

No letter comes, no word of love and cheer for weeks and
    months,
And now another year.

How long, O Lord, how long?
Before the callous grow on tender spots
Where heartaches finally sow.
When love's reward is nought but vain regrets,
Must I grow hard and make myself forget?

How long, O Lord, how long?
While ships delay, my precious years run out,
My powers decay.
My birth-right is lost, by ruthless times decree
To lads, who learned their alphabet from me.
A rusting sword upon a garbage heap,
God give me grace to smile when I would weep eternal justice,

Righter of all wrong,
Dost thou still live,
How long, O Lord, how long?

Jack Edwards recalls:

❛My notes at that time were copied by me on January 14th, 1945. "Six
men have died in four days and the death toll this month is seventy-
two. Two were buried this morning — there are more to go and no
means to stop them dying. One man was killed in the Silo 6. How
long O Lord, how long? As I write, it seems my prayers are being
answered. The air-raid sirens are sounded, maybe our prayers will
be answered soon." As I wrote the above time was 11 o'clock. By 2
o'clock, one more man had died but the American planes were
over.❜

Despite the visible mounting toll of the fire raids and air raids on Japan,
the end of the war came to the Japanese population with dramatic suddenness.

Japan and the world were stunned into a state of peaceful trauma. The B.B.C., in a news bulletin, read out the writing on the wall for Japan:

> ‘Scientists, British and American, have made the atomic bomb at last. The first one was dropped on a Japanese city this morning. It was designed for a detonation equal to 20,000 tons of high explosives. That's 2,000 times the power of one of the R.A.F.'s 10-ton bombs of orthodox design.’

Let a prisoner of war have the last word on this unhappy chapter of events:

> ‘One day when we'd gone back to the main factory, there was a great hullabaloo. All the guards hustled us onto the trains with more haste than they normally do, even for an air-raid, and the doors were shut on us and locked as if it was night and all the camp guards went into the camp office. Well, this of course, was the Imperial message to tell them that the Emperor had decided to quit the war. We, of course, didn't know it. Now previously we had learned that two large bombs had been exploded. One at Nagasaki and one at Hiroshima. That was the first bomb, Nagasaki was the second and we didn't believe the reports that we got from the newspapers which we stole from the factory. That a bomb could kill thousands of people. We just couldn't imagine any bomb large enough to do this, so we said, "Oh, it must be propaganda." Anyway, it was soon after this that the imperial message came through and one day the interpreter said to us. "Well, boys, I've got to go to Tokyo to get some orders, but I think it looks very good for you." So off he went. Two days later he came back and announced to all the prisoners of war of my hut: "Well, boys, the Emperor has decided to drop this useless war and you will all be going home very soon."’

It was to be another two years before some of the Hong Kong lads returned to Hong Kong, but now at least they were free.

12 The Freeing of Hong Kong

The exciting roar of aeroplane engines is heard. A roar, a whoosh of sound. The anxious crowd looking up into the sky can just discern, before the hurtling planes disappear into the horizon, the white star roundels of the United States Air Force. There is a fluttering of white leaves of paper in the air falling to the ground and a flurrying of adults and children scrambling to read the message.

> ❪ Allied POWs and civilian internees, these are your instructions, in case there is capitulation of the Japanese forces.
> 1. You are to remain in your camp area until you receive further instructions from these headquarters.
> 2. Law and order will be maintained in the camp.
> 3. In case of Japanese surrender, there will be Allied occupational troops sent into your camp for your needs and eventual evacuation to your homes.
> 4. You must help by remaining in the area in which you are now located. Your camp leaders we charge with these responsibilities.
> 5. The end is near, do not be disheartened, we are thinking of you. Plans are underway to assist you at the earliest possible moment.
> Signed: A.C. Wedemeyer
> General U.S.E. Commanding ❫

The scene was Stanley camp, although similar enactments of this great moment of excitement took place elsewhere in Hong Kong and Kowloon. Liberation, the end, had already come. Now the prisoners would not be disheartened, but they would become impatient. There was of course a great deal of confusion and uncertainty. This is how John Stericker reacted to the news:

> ❪ I don't know, without the notes in front of me, how long it was before the surrender that the Americans dropped the atom bomb on Japan. We certainly heard of that. I don't think the Japanese local paper they gave us mentioned it. But the news did get through, and

I don't think we were too happy about that because we always thought that they would line us up and shoot us at the end. We thought the atomic bomb might be a very good excuse for doing it. **'**

The Japanese, now that the inevitable had happened, refused at first to accept the full implications of final defeat. Surrender by their Emperor Hirohito, announced to the world by a broadcast, humble and haunted, was incredible. Should they commit hara-kiri, who would receive their Samurai swords as they committed the greatest act of shame? Who would take over authority in Hong Kong? There was a great deal of negotiating and work to be done. It would take time — a fortnight in fact — until the British fleet under the command of Rear Admiral Harcourt sailed into Hong Kong harbour, with the White Ensign and Union Jack flying, and turned a long-cherished dream into reality. From a war correspondent's despatch:

' This was a day to remember — the Jap had been beaten, whether by fair means or foul will be argued for a long while. Idealists were howling that atomic bombs were below the belt. Realists were demanding to know the difference and insisting that if we'd made an ordinary bomb big enough to do the same damage, there would have been no criticism. It occurred to me that justification depends on who uses it. You or the enemy. If he uses it, he's a bastard. If you use it, it's justified.

But that was history and this was 3 o'clock on the afternoon of August 29th, 1945. For two hours we'd been lying off Hong Kong. This was something the thousands of prisoners on Hong Kong would never forget. It was a rainy, leaden, steamy day. It was a day of virtually indescribable joy, tinged with bitterness. A day of tingling excitement and irrepressible impatience. The dawning of a day that would show up the smallness and the greatness of men and women who had waited for three years and eight months of captivity. Through glasses you could see the barracks on Stanley peninsula very plainly. We were so close that, with a little imagination, you could even see people moving around and they could see us. That must have been hard to take but we had to sit there and wait a while yet.

For two days, a strong British force of carriers, cruisers, destroyers, submarines and mine-sweepers commanded by Rear Admiral Harcourt, flying his flag in the aircraft carrier, *HMS Indomitable*, had been beating up through heavily mined waters from Subic Bay in the Philippines. We had brought all the special medical supplies, food, comforts, doctors, nurses and luxuries that could be thrown hastily together in the few hours before the fleet left. The expedition was very aptly named, by someone with a lively sense of humour, Operation Ethelred. That was its official title. The Japanese surrender, like the Japanese entry into the war, had caught us unready and at a bending position. The force had been thrown together overnight. **'**

Bob Clark was an Australian correspondent. coming in with the fleet. He describes first how the British victors met the Japanese conquerors, whose turn it now was to taste bitter humiliation.

' Out on *Indomitable* a reply to the message dropped by G.H.Q. had been received from the Japanese. It said: "Regarding the direct contact between the Japanese authorities and the representatives of the Allied Forces, we have as yet received no instructions from our home government. The Japanese forces in South China, under Lieutenant General Tanaka, are now stationed at Canton and negotiations for cessation of hostilities are directly under the aforesaid General, therefore he is the man to discuss such matters with the representatives of the Allied Forces. Under these circumstances, we regret we cannot send any representatives and wish you to contact him in Canton. We guarantee the safety of any Allied airmen who land in Hong Kong or the New Territories, as well as the safety of personnel already here. We shall communicate with you today by radio on 212 kilocycles. If contact cannot be made on this frequency, 500 kilocycles will be used as stated in your letter of today's date.

Signed: Major General Fukuchi
Chief of Staff," '

In reply to this, Admiral Harcourt sent a message to General Fukuchi in which he said:

> ‘Your message understood. Request you will inform Lieutenant General Tanaka that I intend to enter Hong Kong with a British Squadron on 30th August or 31st August and occupy the naval dockyard, conforming with the Allied Forces' movements with Japan. It will then be possible to discuss arrangements for the surrender and taking control of the Hong Kong area. The final surrender will not take place until after the surrender is signed in Tokyo.’

This was 29 August, when the Liberation fleet had been lying off Hong Kong waters, waiting for the clearing of diplomatic air. Would President Truman back Chiang Kai Shek's own demand to receive the Japanese surrender in Hong Kong and thus enable him to stake his last claim for China? On the very doorstep of Hong Kong, the path for the aircraft carrier and its attendant retinue of cruisers and destroyers had to be cleared of mines, which could have blown the liberators sky-high. In Stanley, Franklin Gimson, the head of the Hong Kong government, was weighing up the risks of premature action, as reported by John Stericker, the Camp Secretary:

> ‘It was most extraordinary because the British love committees and if you have committees they have to be serious. Everything has to be done properly and you sit solemnly and you take notes. Well, I had this ground floor office where we had the weekly, or sometimes twice-weekly, camp committee meetings of all the senior taipans and one or two government officers. I took the minutes. [The office] had a verandah, the doors were open and anybody who was in trouble or wanted to ask me something would come to this verandah. If they saw a meeting on, they usually went away, but on this occasion somebody turned up and leant against the wall. I turned to Franklin Gimson on my right and said, "I'd better go and see what he wants, sir." Meanwhile the committee was gabbling on and I said, "What's the matter?" He said, "The Japanese have surrendered." I said, "Don't talk nonsense. How do you know?" He

said, "Well the Formosan guards have come into the camp and are trying to buy civilian clothes off the internees." So I went back and I whispered in Sir Franklin Gimson's ear that this chap had said they had surrendered. Gimson said to me, as Secretary, "Don't talk nonsense, get on with the meeting." 〞

And this is what Franklin Gimson had to say:

〝 No news of this complete surrender reached Stanley. The wireless sets had long since been confiscated by the Japanese and their operators executed. The English newspaper, for which permission had been given to circulate in the camp, had ceased publication. The news it contained was sparse and repeated the Japanese communiqués, with stories of their triumphs and of the enemy's defeats, so exaggerated as to be incredible. Its stoppage in fact made little difference to the knowledge of the course of the war but severed one of the last links with the outside world. On the plea of gaining instruction in the Japanese language, copies of their newspapers had been obtained and from them detailed study enabled the carefully disguised stories of enemy defeats and of their retreat through Burma and of the American approach to Japan itself to be penetrated. Rumours, of course, circulated, but the more sceptical had learned, through bitter experience, to treat them with suspicion and even ridicule. Then in mid-August 1945, news spread through the camp that the war had ended. No Japanese newspaper appeared to confirm this rumour but gradually more and still more evidence reached Stanley to confirm the apparent truth of the advent of peace. Confidence in the ultimate triumphs of the Allies left no doubt as to who were the victors and that the Japanese, as the vanquished, must pay the penalty of their perfidy and brutality. As the representative of the internees, I considered that some accurate statement was necessary to enable plans to be made for future courses of action and to allay the anxiety from which we were all suffering. I decided therefore to ascertain from the Japanese commandant confirmation or denial of the current rumours. We decided to ask the Japanese to provide accommodation for us in Hong Kong, so as to establish such departments of government as could be satisfactorily manned. Doubts were expressed at the meeting as to whether it would be politic for me to take the oath as officer administering the government, as I was entitled to do, and a decision on this was deferred. Certainly, any disclosure to the Japanese of my assumption of this office might have deterred them from unwittingly extending to me cooperation in furtherance of our plans. I was told of the conclusion of hostilities and the return of peace. Perhaps, rather elated from the altered relationship of captor and captive, I felt is was an occasion to assert my authority by saying, "As senior official of the Hong Kong government I will take charge of the administration". **9**

The Japanese stalled, saying that the future of Hong Kong was not yet decided. There was no certainty it would continue to be British.

6 I replied that this view was merely their expression of opinion with which I was not concerned. I intended to carry out those duties to which I had been appointed by His Majesty's Government. I required accommodation for myself and for my officers and also use of the wireless station. **9**

Now the tenuous vine of the secret network of communications with the outside world began to bear fruit. An emissary of the British Army Aid Group had smuggled himself into Hong Kong and right into the prison camp at Stanley. He brought instructions from London for Mr Gimson.

6 I returned to my quarters and, while again thinking of what the future might portend, a knock sounded on the door and a Chinese entered with an air of a conspirator making a secret rendezvous. He asked me if I were Mr Gimson and, when I said I was, he gave me a short account of the international scene, consequent to the victory of the Allies and the defeat of the Japanese. What I learnt carried the firm conviction that I should take the oath as officer administering the government and proclaim to the world I had done so.

A meeting was immediately summoned of a few of the leading personnel in Stanley and the Chief Justice of the Colóny, Sir Athol MacGregor, administered to me the oath of office. Thus I became what was virtually Acting Governor of Hong Kong.

After the meeting, when my visitor and I were left alone, he again asked me if I wanted any money. From a bag poured a quantity of golden sovereigns. I took five, more as a momento of the occasion rather than for any personal needs. In internment, money had usually been associated with blackmarket transactions and perhaps the sight of a legitimate currency was too much of a shock for me to appreciate its value, in a world where food would no longer be supplied as a ration from an alien authority. A message of my assumption of duties had to be conveyed to His Majesty's Government, but the only possible means of communication available to us to convey this information was to be found in Macau. Even then, the journey there presented grave difficulties. A volunteer bravely offered to undertake it in a Chinese fishing boat. He was sucessful in his mission, but on his way back was intercepted by a pirate vessel. The volunteer, to escape attention in the search which followed, was hidden in a pile of dried fish and was very nearly asphyxiated in consequence. He was luckily not discovered and returned to tell the tale. 9

This was Arthur May; the Chinese emissary was Phoenix, Colonel Ride's link man in Macau, who was awarded the C.B.E. for these highly important services. Meanwhile, in Shamshuipo and in Central, the ever energetic Selwyn-Clarke was taking a hand in the making of history.

6 After nearly four years under a foreign power it seemed to some of us, in the flood of feeling that this moment released, that those who might come to liberate the Colony ought to find the British flag flying. The internees asked me to assume control of the camp. Arthur May produced a Union Jack which he had concealed, at considerable danger to himself, throughout the occupation, and Hilda, it was suggested, should have the honour of hoisting it on a

long bamboo pole. The little ceremony had only just been completed when the guards came rushing from their headquarters and ordered me to lower the flag. This I refused to do without a personal written order from the Japanese Military Governor so that I should have something to show to the liberating force when it arrived. The guards departed and the flag remained flying.

At 2 p.m. next day, however, they returned with an order in Chinese characters and a typewritten translation with the Governor's chop or signature stating that the Japanese military government was still in charge of the camp. This was technically correct and I did not want to expose the camp residents to some retaliatory outburst. The gesture had been made and I prolonged it a little by insisting that it was not the British custom to lower the flag before the hour of retreat, which in Hong Kong was 6.30 p.m. At dusk that evening I reluctantly told Arthur that the flag must come down and it did. ›

Not only the Japanese found it hard to comprehend the new set of circumstances. For the POWs there was incredulity and jubilation. There was joy, although Private Gomez was to discover on going home for the first time in nearly four years that joy was mingled with sadness at what the Japanese had done to his father, suspected of being a British spy.

‹ We got news about the liberation one day when we were off on a working party. I remember quite clearly my aunt was on the roadside and she shouted to us that the war was over, the Japanese had surrendered. That night, when we went back to camp, there was tremendous elation but there was a nagging doubt as to whether or not it was true. A couple of days later of course it turned out to be true and in due course we were allowed to go home. My own home-coming was not all happiness because my father had been taken by the Japanese into Stanley prison as a suspected spy and the poor man was subjected to all sorts of tortures, water torture, electric torture, and the crucifix torture. We were not sure whether he had been executed or whether he was alive and well. It wasn't until many days afterwards that we heard from him. Of course then it was all joy. ›

Things were on the move, however, to bring the uncertainty to an end. Gimson was now in the French Mission building, surrounded by his embryonic administration, but he had to depend upon the Japanese forces to keep law and order against the waves of Chinese looting and people exacting retribution against the Kempeitai.

‘After ten days or so of mounting anxiety I called on the Japanese liaison officer to enquire if he had heard any news of the approach of the relieving forces. By good chance a message had just been received, stating that a British plane would be landing at Kai Tak Aerodrome at a specified time and date and that a Japanese officer should be present to be conveyed back to the aircraft carrier to receive instructions regarding the entry into the harbour of the British fleet. I then said, "Of course you are complying with this order." The Japanese replied, "No. We have no authority to negotiate. A message is to be sent, the dispatch of this plane would serve no useful purpose and so entry would be refused." This position I was not prepared to accept. "The plane," I retorted, "should land to embark an officer, whom I wish to convey to the Admiral commanding the fleet information regarding the situation in Hong Kong."
I was then told an excuse that Kai Tak was under water and that a plane could not land. This argument had to be withdrawn when I pointed out that there had been no rain for three weeks. After further discussion, I felt I must assert my authority. "A paragraph must be added at the conclusion of the message you are going to send that I had directed the plane should land to meet an officer designated by me and to convey him to the flag ship. You have refused. Details of this refusal must be inserted in your message. Omission to do so, as well as your attitude with regard to the landing of the plane at Kai Tak, will be treated as offences triable by a criminal court." The Japanese's reaction to this was to consult his Chief of Staff. He returned soon after to say that he would meet the plane and proceed to the aircraft carrier for instructions. He did so, accompanied by the naval officer attached to my administration. Unfortunately, the plane conveying this Japanese officer on his

155

return flight to Hong Kong had to make a forced landing in territory occupied by Chinese guerrillas, who immediately surrounded it, seizing the Japanese with the declared intention of cutting his throat. The British pilot protested that the Japanese was his prisoner and then was immediately handed a knife with the words "Here, take this and you cut his throat." **>**

Correspondent Clark again takes up the story:

< A further message was received by radio telephone from the Colony that a Commander Craven, R.N., would like to come on board with one other. As a result of this message, an Avenger with an escort of four Hell Cats took off for Kai Tak airfield. When it came back the Avenger was met on the flight deck by a Captain and a Sergeant of Marines, both carrying sten guns. The Jap envoy started to get up. That was Makamura, a slight, dapper little civilian, who had been head of the Japanese foreign office in the Colony. He made a bad entrance, losing a great deal of face in the process. He was all dressed up for the occasion: gold braid, badges, breeches, jack-boots, a may-west and a sword. It was the mae west and the sword that beat him. The sword was more than half his own length. The may-west gave him twice his normal bulk. He got stuck, then he got himself tangled, then he got both tangled and stuck. The marines prised him loose and he hopped down, clutching his sword tightly in his hot little hand, and saluted. Makamura was taken to the carrier's 'island'. The door closed behind him. A marine guard paced up and down outside. He wanted to see Admiral Harcourt but Harcourt had no intention of seeing him so he had to be content with Captain Eccles, captain of *Indomitable*. Eccles and Makamura were going to see a lot of each other in the weeks ahead. The second man to get out of the plane was Commander Craven. He was immediately surrounded by several officers who served with him before he was taken prisoner and the Admiral saw him immediately on the bridge. While all this was going on, a message was received from the Admiralty giving the text of a signal they had picked up from Mr Gimson, the British Colonial Secretary in Hong Kong before the

Japanese occupation. In it Gimson said he had already prepared a complete scheme for setting up civil administration in the Colony, including the New Territories. The Secretary, in his message, told Mr Gimson that his offer had been passed to Rear Admiral Harcourt who was to establish military administration by proclamation. "You should comply fully with his instructions," added the Secretary, and Gimson did. He and all the other Colony public servants, sick and tired though they were, went straight from internment into harness again. **'**

Then came the final act in this drama, on 30 August:

' Towards midday we began moving. The mine-sweepers went up to the head of the column and headed for Tat On channel. After the mine-sweepers came the destroyer, *Kempenfeldt*, then the cruiser *Swiftsure*, to which Admiral Harcourt had transferred his flag. After *Swiftsure* came another destroyer, *Euryalus*, then *Prince Robert*. Bringing up the rear was the depot ship *Maidstone*. That was the beginning of one of the toughest, happiest, craziest days of my life. We crept in through Lye Mun pass, which is only a couple of hundred yards wide. It was here that the first Jap swam across from the mainland to Hong Kong Island. On the rocks, a coolie whistled shrilly. It was like an obscenity in that stillness. Then we were in Victoria Harbour and still there was no movement. Sunken Japanese shipping lay half submerged all over the harbour; even on shore there seemed to be little sign of activity. There was not a launch or a sampan moving on the water. A few Chinese, not more than about fifty, stood on the waterfront opposite the Peninsula Hotel, watching. We warped into our berth in Kowloon and tied up. The Chinese clapped and cheered. It was a watery reception and made practically no impression on the oppressive silence. It was like entering a near dead city. An American civilian came running onto the jetty. He threw out his arms. Tears were streaming down his face and he was crying, "Thank God you've come at last. We've had four years of hell. I tell you, the bastards have given us hell." His Eurasian wife stood beside him, impassive, unmoved. We, on the ship, did not know what to do. We could not stand there watching him we couldn't turn away — there was nothing to say, the gang planks weren't down yet, he could not come on board. No one could go down to him and you could find no words to say to a man who is standing in front of you crying. Then the planks were down and we went ashore. People began to arrive on the dock — just a dribble: a couple of Indian Army officers were first. Their uniforms were very clean, very neatly pressed and painstakingly patched. You did not have to be told that they had been hoarding them for this day. Their eyes were very bright, glistening, and they walked straight and very proudly. A group of Indians arrived and out of their eyes shone that same overwhelming gladness. There is a degree of happiness that hurts and I never knew it until that day. **>**

Who should have the last word about this momentous episode in the history of Hong Kong? My vote is for Selwyn-Clarke, who not only resisted the enemy, but who also revealed that spirit of saintliness which transcends even the glories of patriotism.

< The feeling was of air coming back into one's lungs; of a huge weight being lifted from one's chest. **>**

And John Stericker, who had kept sane among the petty insanities of Stanley, was proud too.

< One of the first things I did when Sir Cecil Harcourt arrived was to be sent back to the Z.B.W. Hong Kong radio station at Gloucester Building. There I found the studio completely unchanged; the same microphone, everything was there, just as we had left it. Just as before the surrender I had been the radio announcer who brought his Excellency, Sir Mark Young, to the microphone to say it was all over, bar the shouting, I had the great triumph of re-opening radio Hong Kong by announcing His Excellency, Admiral Sir Cecil Harcourt, Governor of Hong Kong, to say we'd won it all back again. **>**

Liberation

(XXIII – XXXIVb)

XXIII. The effective liberation of Hong Kong took place in the first week of September when British Naval Forces followed in the wake of the flagship of the Commander of the Task Force. Rear Admiral Sir Cecil Harcourt, who sailed into Victoria Harbour in H.M.S. *Swiftsure* on 30th August 1945. (*Lady May Ride*)

XXIV. The Naval Headquarters were located in the Peninsula Hotel, Kowloon and in the first few days, communications between Headquarters and Hong Kong Island were by means of naval cutters, shown here in convoy, making their way across the narrow stretch of water between Tsimshatsui and the Naval Dockyard.   (*Imperial War Museum, London*)

XXV. The entry of the Navy into the harbour had been cautious on account of suspected minefields and the presence of 'kamekaze' crews of Japanese torpedo boats operating from Lamma Island. It was necessary for the Navy to round up these Japanese sailors, who, it was thought, might make a last minute resistance to the British despite the Imperial Rescript issued in Tokyo on 14th August. (*Imperial War Museum, London*)

XXVI. The Imperial Japanese Army was compliant enough, fearful as they were of the vengeful local population. Moreover, at first, in the absence of the 3rd Commando Brigade to enforce law and order among the lynching and looting mob, the Hong Kong Government, which emerged out of the Stanley Internment Camp ahead of the arrival of Harcourt and his Force, relied upon the reluctant efforts of Japanese troops to prevent total anarchy in the Colony. Eventually, there were sufficient British troops to take up this responsibility and the Japanese military were marched out of their own barracks into Shamshuipo, now cleared of British prisoners of war.

(Imperial War Museum, London)

XXVII. This picture shows British officers conferring with a Japanese counterpart (still wearing his sword) about arrangements at Kaitak.

(*Imperial War Museum, London*)

XXVIII. At Stanley the Navy was greeted with open arms. Here was the real liberation. The bitter past was put aside; there were services of thanksgiving at having survived the rigours of captivity. The Union Jack was ceremoniously run up.

(Imperial War Museum, London)

XXIX. Franklin C. Gimson. the chief Hong Kong Government representative in Stanley Camp. reporting to Rear
Admiral Sir Cecil Harcourt   (*Lady May Ride*)

XXX. There was a political side to the liberation more complicated than the simple issue of freeing people from captivity.

The Japanese local commanders had to sign Deeds of Surrender to the Representatives of the victorious Allied Powers.

This was an opportunity for Chiang Kai-shek to make a last minute attempt to assert his authority over Hong Kong and a bid to the major Allied Power, the United States, to eject the British.

This diplomatic move was unsuccessful; however, it delayed the formal ceremony of surrender at Government House until 16th September 1945.   (*Public Archives, Canada*)

XXXI. Rear-Admiral-Harcourt inspecting the guard of honour for the Japanese surrender ceremony at Government House. *(Public Archives, Canada)*

XXXII. Raising the Union Jack at Government House during the Japanese surrender ceremony.

(Public Archives, Canada)

XXXIII. Signing of the Japanese surrender at Government House.   (*Public Archives, Canada*)

XXXIV. a. Victory Parade. March past in front of the Hongkong and Shanghai Banking Corporation.

(*Imperial War Museum, London*)

XXXIV. b. When the diplomatic haggles had been settled it was time to demonstrate to the people of Hong Kong that Hong Kong was a British colony again at a Victory Parade. The Chinese and British flags flew together on this rare occasion.

(*Imperial War Museum, London*)

13 All the Tea in China

Among the records of relief and jubilation is this:

> ‘I was on a ferry going to Shamshuipo and it was the day when we used to go to give the prisoners of war their parcels. With me I had a Russian girl and a French girl. A young man came and went to my Russian friend. He was Russian himself, and said, "Everything is over." I heard that and I was so startled I started to cry; I couldn't help it, it was so over-coming. My French friend said, "What's the matter? What bad news has she given you?" I said, "He's told me that everything was over." She said, "Well, rejoice, don't cry." I said, "But I'm rejoicing, it's my way of rejoicing, I am so happy."’

That was a French lady who had not been interned in Stanley. One of the Shamshuipo prisoner's reminiscences reveals how immersed the captives had become in their petty preoccupations. Then liberation and sanity broke in:

> ‘We had already heard rumours of a very vague nature, but there was no clear evidence of hostilities coming to an end. In the hut in which I was living, we had this curious incident, namely that one of the sentries was in the course of having a tremendous argument with an officer who could talk good Japanese.
>
> This argument, we knew, was over the subject of the price of wool as many of us had sacrificed our socks and other garments for the sales through this particular man. In the midst of it we asked the officer to enquire what the position was, and to our astonishment the sentry curtly said, "Yes, the war is over."
>
> I had no thoughts that surrender was so near. In fact at the beginning of the summer, I'd followed my usual practice of going to the barbers and having all my hair chopped off to a very short length, although the barber, who was Major Jack Watson, said to me, "You're making a grave mistake in having all your hair taken off because we shall be out before the end of the summer." He said this

regularly and I took no notice of it at all. I had all my hair taken off, it was nice and cool and clean. **'**

There was to be an amusing sequel to this sign of refusal to believe in the possibility of this strange world coming to an end. This Volunteer was one of the two or three thousand survivors of the horrors of Shamshuipo. At last they were free, even if they still had to muster in the mornings. At least the orders could now be given in English. The local lads also wanted to visit their loved ones in Stanley and our friend, who had smartened himself up in an over enthusiastic manner, was in for a shock when he crossed to the Island and eventually found his wife.

> **'**The most exciting of the whole business was the news that husbands, fathers, and fiancées were going to be allowed to go to Stanley to see their wives, families and girlfriends. And so one bright morning we went through the gates there, through the barbed-wire gates and jumped off this lorry, I looking around for my wife. There was no wife to be seen but somebody pushed a young chap into my arms and said, "There's your son," and there, for the first time, I saw this young men, of three and a half years old, who had been born so shortly after we went into imprisonment and then I heard that my wife was in hospital, so I moved on with my son to Tweed Bay Hospital. There, I went up the stairs, and at the entrance to the ward I was told to wait, because they were putting screens around my wife's bed. It was a very exciting, a very happy, a very tense moment and I remember the nursing sisiter standing there telling me to calm myself down, to quiet myself. However, when they'd finished putting the screens around my wife's bed, I went into her ward. Then she saw me and said in accents charged with emotion, "What have they done to your hair?" **'**

Throughout Hong Kong, in and out of the camps, there would be scenes of pathos and, now that people could smile, humour as well. Another inmate of Stanley recalls how her young son announced the glad news to his mother.

> **'**I was in Stanley Camp, living in an amah's room with my small son

of three and a half. Christopher came in one morning and said, "Mummy, the naughty war is open." He'd got mixed up with the war being over and the camp being open, but he said, "It is true, because Christopher Potter told me." Christopher Potter was four.'

In Stanley the flag was raised and there was a memorial service of thanksgiving and remembrance for those who would forever remain at Stanley in the peaceful cemetery. Admiral Harcourt and his flag officers visited the camp, bringing food and clothing in jeeps, a sight never before seen in Hong Kong. Here, at first, there was celebration. It was only later as the slow wheels of bureaucracy — British this time — wore down the patience of internees, that the long pent-up feelings of captivity flared up. Liberation was now the reality, not the dream of paradise. The process of liberation was in fact a long drawn-out affair and amongst the military, better disciplined perhaps than the civilians of Stanley, there was at Shamshuipo, as Lieutenant Wright recalls, almost a sombre note to proceedings.

'You stayed in the prison camp for another fortnight and then you were only allowed out in organized parties to get food or something of that sort.'

Was it a cause for celebration? Was there a general atmosphere of relief?

'Oh, of relief; I wouldn't say celebration. I think of just relief almost at first and then relief certainly. There was no violent cheering or people going mad or anything like that. I think people were too numbed in a way to be able to react. If one reacted at all, and I can only talk for myself, one tended to burst into tears rather than cheer and laugh.'

Of course, it was difficult for the Japanese to believe that now they would have to change places with their prisoners behind the barbed-wire. Colonel Bothelo:

'We were told that the Japanese Emperor was going to make a big announcement the following day, and at a certain time the Japanese all had had to parade and the camp was practically devoid of guards. They had all had to assemble to hear this great announcement. So, at that time, we very definitely knew that Japan had surrendered. So much so that, on the following morning when we had the usual roll-call, and the Japanese camp commandant came to count us; Colonel Simon White said, "Well, we refuse to be counted because the war is over and we have won the war." The camp commandant replied he didn't know anything about it. Typically Japanese, he hummed and hawed and kept on sucking his teeth — he didn't know anything about it, you see — so the Camp Colonel Simon White took him into his office and showed him a copy of a Chinese paper which had been smuggled into camp. "Here is the news." And he said, Oh, well, he hadn't confirmation, that he would have to find out. He went away — he didn't count us — and came back later to confirm the news that Japan had surrendered and that Colonel Simon White then was to maintain law and order in camp. Subsequently, a flight of American planes, B28s or something like that, I can't remember the name, flew over the camp and dropped messages, signed by General Wedemeyer, which said we were to remain in camp until we were relieved. We then mounted our own guards, so to speak, to see that prisoners of war didn't leave camp, more for their sake than anything else; because there was an instance where someone was so happy about it, he rushed into the Medical Inspection room and drank a bottle of ethyl alcohol and died. We mounted our own guards and then there were some . . . What shall I say? . . . What's the word, now? Turncoats in camp. And we had . . . the Commandant had to see that they weren't manhandled, you see. **'**

There were ceremonial parades. The hoisting of the Union Jack and the playing of the British National Anthem symbolized this reassertion of the British Empire. Even the most case-hardened in this crucible of captivity were touched, as Dr S.M. Bard recalls:

' The most solemn and proudest occasion of the days as a prisoner of war was the morning when the whole camp was paraded and every prisoner went to great effort to produce his best uniform which was already in rags. Sam Browns were polished, boots were polished and brasses were polished and the whole camp marched on parade with the camp band leading.

That was a very touching ceremony. I must admit a certain amount of cynicism but I was really touched. Once we got the Japanese sentries out of the camp and they agreed to stay out, we raised the flag — an old Union Jack appeared from somewhere, somebody had had it hidden all the time. And up it went. There was deadly silence and I distinctly remember quite a number of men with tears in their eyes. We were still completely alone on the Island with no fleet in sight. **)**

But for the men and women in the street — the Chinese — feelings were much more explosive.

(Our food was so scarce and precious that although you hated to lose a pound of bread, when you saw the man who had snatched it off your hands running along and tearing the paper with his teeth and eating it there and then, somehow you felt he needed it more than you did.

When the war ended, I was just nine years old. The only thing that frightened me was when, just after the war, cakes, European-type cakes, first came out, and my mother took me to a shop and we got some. I was carrying a bag of cakes and swinging it along, and suddenly a beggar came up to me and just grabbed the whole thing and stuffed the thing in his mouth, bag and all. He just ate it next to me! Of course, I was so dumbfounded, that I stood still and he stood still, next to me, and in no time the whole thing disappeared into his mouth. **)**

Some years earlier when some of the prisoners had gone out in the streets of Kowloon on their way to work at Kai Tak, they had remarked that the Chinese were an undemonstrative race. But now there was the opportunity to take the law into one's own hands, to loot and steal even from one's own kind,

174

and to deal with the hated Japanese gendarmerie who had kept Hong Kong quiet under a vicious rule of terror. Some of the Japanese would not survive the war after all. One of the "local" prisoners of war who had gone into town witnessed these acts of vengeance.

> ‘There were still trams running. The Chinese people stopped all the trams that passed the dockyard and they'd go up to each tram, search it and pull out the Japanese people from the tram. And they were searched for their valuables and then tortured in the streets. One Japanese, whom the Chinese recognized as one of the gendarmes, was tortured to death at the main gate.’

But, slowly, things returned to normal and there was now a British head of the military administration resident in Government House. It was here that the Japanese left their lasting mark on Hong Kong. In place of the old crumbling building in Upper Albert Road, opposite the Botanical Gardens, the Japanese constructed a replica of an ancient stronghold, a donjon with curved roofs and stupas on those roofs.

John Stericker was to come out of Stanley to become a broadcaster again and introduce Franklin Gimson to the microphone, when he made his farewell address to Hong Kong.

> ‘It is with feelings of both joy and sorrow that I take this opportunity of addressing a few farewell words to listeners in Hong Kong. Of joy, that we have come through the worst tribulations of the war and are free men again. And of sorrow, that I leave you with my normal mission, as a professional colonial administrator, unfulfilled because of the upheavals of war. You of my listeners who so loyally and zealously supported me in the immediate job of keeping the Colony going, pending the arrival of his Excellency the Commander-in-Chief, have now seen the Prime Minister's message of warm appreciation of your efforts. Friday's proclamation, appointing the Chief Civil Affairs Officer under the Commander-in-Chief's administration will relieve many of you at an early date to take a well-earned rest in your homelands. Some of you may remain for

some time longer and I know that those who do so will continue to give the Chief Civil Affairs Officer all the assistance in your power. I trust that those of you who stay behind for some time will enjoy health and strength to assist the new administration to lay well the foundations of the future prosperity of the Colony and its people.

But there are others in the Colony to whom some expression of the gratitude which we, who were interned, feel towards them is long overdue. I refer to some of our fellow nationals of the Chinese, Portuguese, and Indian communities who were left behind to bear the brunt of the Japanese oppression in Hong Kong and who in spite of persecution and privations, and in some cases even taking the extreme forms of torture and imprisonment, refused to do anything which would injure the cause of the United Nations, but rather did their utmost to promote it by any means in their power. Some of us who were shut in behind barbed wire will never forget the assistance we got from many such kindly people, who with grave risk, heavy expense and much self-denial, sent parcels of supplies to us which may truly be said in many cases to have made all the difference between comparative good health and permanent disablement or even death. Since our release, the faithful coöperation of these loyal people has contributed materially to the smooth resumption of normal life here. It is my earnest hope that all who have behaved so nobly will regain their former livelihood and re-establish themselves, either in their private business or in the public service on a sound basis of prosperity, and that the government will do its utmost to assist in the restoration of such people to their rightful places in the life of the community.

In conclusion, I can only express regret that my time in Hong Kong has been spent in the midst of circumstances of unparalleled distress and calamity for the whole of the population and that I was rendered personally so powerless, but I can assure you that though perforce out of contact with the populace and the territory of the Colony, I have been giving constant thought and spending much of my time in internment to discussions as to the means whereby the political, social and economic conditions of the people here might be reformed and bettered. **'**

John Stericker describes further how Government House was transformed by the Japanese Governors Isogai and Tanaka. It was here, too, that the famous Stanley tiger had been stuffed and used as a symbol of the occupiers' ferocity in dealing with resistance to the false empire of Asian co-prosperity.

> **'** Being secretary to the camp, I was one of the first people who met Admiral Sir Cecil Harcourt who was the new Governor of Hong Kong and I had to show him round the camp and he shook hands with lots of people and I got to know him very well and sort of became unofficial A.D.C. to him on the civilian side, once we went back into Hong Kong. The only surprising thing was the Japanese had re-built Government House and re-built it very well. The whole of one floor had been turned into a Japanese shrine. It was the most marvellous place — all tatami on the floor and shrines. It was completely Japanese. **'**

In Government House on 16 September the once proud Japanese Commanders signed the Deed of Surrender, bringing a formal end to the Japanese occupation of Hong Kong and, at the same time, recognizing that once more Hong Kong was a British Colony. That Deed read:

> **'** We, Major General Umekichi Okada and Vice-Admiral Ruitaro Fujita, in virtue of the unconditional surrender to the Allied Powers of all Japanese armed forces and all forces under Japanese control wherever situated, as proclaimed in Article 2 of the Instrument of Surrender, signed in Tokyo Bay on the 2nd of September, 1945 on behalf of the Emperor of Japan and the Japanese Imperial Head-quarters, do hereby unconditionally surrender ourselves and all forces under our control to Rear Admiral Cecil Halliday Jephson Harcourt, C.B., C.B.E. and undertake to carry out all such instruc-tions as may be given by him or under his authority and to issue all necessary orders for the purpose of giving effect to all his instructions. Given under our hands, this 16th day of September, 1945, at Government House, Hong Kong. **'**

If Hong Kong was now a Colony with a future of prosperity, that prosperity depended upon the character of the Hong Kong people who, in the words of Jean Gittins, had withstood these vicissitudes of war with fortitude.

'Everything became a community effort. No one could have dreamt that we would have been so adaptable. Those who were not so inclined by nature acquired the habit in order to survive. A few, who could not or would not, simply died. Seasons came and went and Christmas, followed each Easter, and Easters succeeded every Christmas, and we drifted imperceptibly from one year into the next. It was as well that we did not know of the shortages we would have to suffer, nor of how long our internment would last. Strength seemed to grow from within us as we faced each new problem firm in our conviction that it would somehow be solved, and we found a faith that fortified our resilience and leant support to our fortitude. There is an old Chinese saying that heaven never drives a man to desperation. Happily our trust in heaven was never misplaced. It would only be fair to add, however, that desperate as our plight seemed to be at the time, we found when the war was over that many other camps had suffered hardships and privations far greater than ours. The large numbers who succumbed to malnutrition and disease in Shamshuipo, Hainan and Singapore, to name a few of the POW camps, and the pitiful state of many of those who managed to survive, made light of our situation. Above all, the poignant stories told by returning prisoners from Japan showed how relatively fortunate we, in Stanley, had been.'

These captive years, were they a complete waste of lives? The future of Hong Kong hung in the balance during four years, it is true. The agonies, the sufferings, the privations were gone through as history took its course, and as men and women made that history. These experiences are summed up by one man, Bob Yates, a regular soldier and a prisoner of war in Hong Kong and Japan:

'Being a regular soldier I left Britain on November 16th, 1935 and I had been to Gibraltar and Egypt before going to Hong Kong. When

I got back on November 13th 1945, I'd been away ten years and two weeks without a break. When I left, my sisters were going to school, When I came back, well, two of them were married.

We knew nothing about the latest pop songs — in those days we called them hits. We knew none of the songs. We knew nothing or very little about what had gone on, and so when you got into conversation with someone you felt completely lost. For example, if you were talking about a football match between Liverpool and Everton in 1943 or '44, they'd say, "You remember when so and so scored that goal!" Of course, you hadn't seen the match, you didn't even know the result, you hadn't heard about it so you absolutely lost the conversation. The only conversation you could have with people who hadn't been there was rationing, which of course everybody could talk about, and the weather, which every Englishman talks about anyway. That was about all. It was just as if you'd had four years sliced out of your life. For example, the simple things like GI. We didn't know what a GI was.

I don't tend to be philosophical really but I found that you see the worst in human nature in those circumstances and you see the very best. I'm glad to say that the very best in people comes out far more often than the very worst.

There was the odd chap who would rob a dying man of his last cigarette. On the other hand, I've known people who would nurse and look after their mates. This to me is very important. This spirit lives on now through our Association where we have a reunion at the Festival Hall every October. We go along there and nobody's talking about the bad times. You know, there's peals of laughter when they're talking about things that happened that were funny, and there were funny things that happened.

I've often said to people, and this sounds contradictory I know, "I wouldn't have missed it for all the tea in China." That's about the best way I can sum it up. **>**

Bibliography and Sources Quoted

The war in Hong Kong, 1941–1945, is not forgotten or dead. Almost every month sees the publication of accounts of the battle, and now even novels based upon wartime incidents (e.g. Robert Gandt's *Season of Storms*, SCMP, 1982, and Anthony Esler's *Bastion*, London, 1980).

The following list and comments are not intended to be a complete bibliography of this growing number of books on the subject. The focus of this list is for the purpose of documenting, wherever possible, the quotations and narrative used in the original radio programmes. This means, of course, that the 'standard' documents and histories of the campaign and its aftermath are purposely omitted. The details of these are given in *Hong Kong Eclipse*.

There are no known 'official' records of the occupation in Hong Kong. The official transcript of the trial of General Rensuke Isogai, the first Japanese Governor of the Occupied Territory, which took place in Nanking, and which relied on testimony collected by Allied War Crimes Teams in postwar Hong Kong, has not been traced. There are scanty Office of Strategic Services reports made to the U.S. Government, reporting the structure of administration in Hong Kong, which are reproduced in *Hong Kong Eclipse*.

Although the Hong Kong Government maintained a semblance of continuity in the Stanley Internment Camp and there are some records of its underground control of the internees, these are necessarily fragmentary. Those that survive have been collected in John Stericker's unpublished history of the Camp and its administration, 'Captive Colony', and a summary account is given in his book, *A Tear for the Dragon*. There is also a collection of Gimson papers in the Public Records Office, Hong Kong. These have been consulted.

The Japanese administration apparently destroyed its records before the British returned in 1945. From the Japanese point of view there is one handbook on Hong Kong (in Japanese) compiled in 1944 which gives a directory of the machinery of occupation. It has not been necessary to quote from that volume, Koji Saito, *Hong Kong under military administration*, Hong Kong, 1944.

Allowing for the inevitable propaganda slant, the best source for descriptions of everyday life in Hong Kong in the years 1942–1945 is the *Hong*

Kong News. This presumably was published mainly for the benefit of the English-reading Third Nationals in Hong Kong and it also found its way to the internees. The leading Chinese newspaper, *Wah Kiu Yat Po*, continued publication throughout the war and some accounts from it have been used.

There are several first-hand Chinese accounts of life under the Japanese occupation, some of which were consulted in translation for the writing of the radio programmes. Several have been discovered since the listing of the then known titles in the bibliography to *Hong Kong Eclipse*. The interested researcher is directed to the catalogue of the Hong Kong Collection in the University of Hong Kong Library.

ALAN BIRCH

Published Works

Andrea [Dorothy Jenner], as told to Trish Sheppard. *Darlings, I've had a Ball!* Sydney: Ure Smith, 1975.

Birch, Alan and G.B. Endacott. *Hong Kong Eclipse*. Hong Kong: Oxford University Press, 1978.

Bush, Lewis. *Clutch of Circumstance*. Tokyo, 1956.

Carew, Tim *Hostages to Fortune*. London: Hamish Hamilton, 1971.

Clark, R.S. *An End to Tears*. Adelaide: Peter Huston, 1946.

Dew, Gwen. *Prisoner of the Japanese*. New York: A.A. Knopf, 1943.

Garneau, Grant S. *The Royal Rifles of Canada in Hong Kong, 1941–5*. Quebec: Hong Kong Veterans of Canada, Maritime Branch, 1980.

Gittins, Jean. *I was at Stanley*. Hong Kong: Ye Olde Printerie, 1946.

Goodwin, Ralph. *Hong Kong Escape*. London: Arthur Barker, 1953.

Guest, Freddie. *Escape from the Bloodied Sun*. London: Hutchinson, 1956.

Hahn, Emily. *China to Me*. Philadelphia: Blakiston Press Co., 1949.

Hamilton, G.C. *The Sinking the of* [sic] *Lisbon Maru*. Hong Kong: Green Pagoda Press, 1966.

Harrop, Phyllis R. *Hong Kong Incident*. London: Eyre & Spottiswoode, 1943.

Li Shu-fan. *Hong Kong Surgeon*. New York: Dutton, 1964.

Lindsay, Oliver. *At the Going Down of the Sun*. London: Hamish Hamilton, 1981.

Luff, John. *The Hidden Years*. Hong Kong: South China Morning Post, 1967.

Priestwood, Gwen, *Through Japanese Barbed Wire*. London: Appleton-Century-Croft. 1943.

Proulx, B.A. *Underground from Hong Kong*. New York: E.P. Dutton Co., 1943.

Ride, Edwin. *BAAG: Hong Kong Resistance 1942–1945*. Hong Kong: Oxford University Press, 1981.

Selwyn-Clarke, Sir Selwyn. *Footprints*. Hong Kong: Sino-American Press, 1975.

Sewell, W.G. *Strange Harmony*. London: Edinburgh House Press, 1948.

Skvorzov, A.V. *Chinese Ink and Brush Sketches of Prisoner of War Camp Life in Hong Kong, 25 December, 1941–30 August, 1945*. Hong Kong, 1948.

Stericker, J. *A Tear for the Dragon*. London: Arthur Barker, 1958.

Ward, R.S., *Asia for the Asiatics? The Techniques of Japanese Occupation*. Chicago: University of Chicago Press, 1945.

Zia, I.D. *The Unforgettable Epoch 1937–1945*. Hong Kong: Greenwood Press, 1969.

Unpublished works

Bourke, Revd. Fr., S.J. 'Steering neutral in troubled waters', Hong Kong: 1941–45.

Castro, F.M. (Sonny). 'Broadcast talks on life in Shamshiupo P.O.W. Camp'. (Personal Ms.).

Chatley, W.H.P., Lt. 'Report on wireless activities in Stanley'. (Public Records Office of Hong Kong).

Dudley, Marion, 'Hong Kong prison camp'. (Typescript, New York Public Library, 1942?).

Gimson, F.C. 'Diary, February 1942–June 1943'. (Public Records Office, Hong Kong).

Gittins, J. 'Through trials to triumph'.

Hong Kong Occupied Territory, Governor's Office, Press Division. 'Record of a press conference by several Japanese who had lived in Hong Kong at the outbreak of World War II and who were interned in Stanley.' Hong Kong, December 1942.

Radio-Television Hong Kong. Various interviews from the programme. 'Unhappy Chapter', broadcast in 1961. No interviewees are identified.

The Japanese surrender
of Hong Kong
16th September 1945